Quarterly Essay

T5-CGA-875

Quarterly Essay is published four times a year by Black Inc., an imprint of Schwartz Media Pty Ltd. Publisher: Morry Schwartz.

ISBN 978-1-86395-616-1 ISSN 1832-0953

Subscriptions – 1 year (4 issues): $59 within Australia incl. GST. Outside Australia $89.
2 years (8 issues): $105 within Australia incl. GST. Outside Australia $165.

Payment may be made by Mastercard or Visa, or by cheque made out to Schwartz Media. Payment includes postage and handling.

To subscribe, fill out and post the subscription card or form inside this issue, or subscribe online:

www.quarterlyessay.com
subscribe@blackincbooks.com
Phone: 61 3 9486 0288

Correspondence should be addressed to:

The Editor, Quarterly Essay
37–39 Langridge Street
Collingwood VIC 3066 Australia
Phone: 61 3 9486 0288 / Fax: 61 3 9486 0244
Email: quarterlyessay@blackincbooks.com

Editor: Chris Feik. Management: Sophy Williams, Caitlin Yates. Publicity: Anna Lensky. Design: Guy Mirabella. Assistant Editor/Production Coordinator: Nikola Lusk. Typesetting: Duncan Blachford.

Printed by Griffin Press, Australia. The paper used to produce this book comes from wood grown in sustainable forests.

To my sisters. Magnificent women.

THE PRINCE | Faith, *Abuse and George Pell*

David Marr

THE ONLY CAB ON THE RANK

The cardinal was floundering. "I don't think we should be scapegoated. We'll answer for what we've done, for … what we've done. We're not trying to defend the indefensible. But let's …" He paused. "Right across the board … let's see." By turns he was weary and defiant. He complained. He wandered off into the far reaches of Catholic history. Once mentioned, the victims were all but forgotten. Journalists crowded into that plain room in Polding House could not believe what they were seeing. This man had been a bishop for twenty-five years, a cardinal for ten, archbishop in turn of Australia's two biggest cities and a big figure in Rome since the time of John Paul II. He had faced tough press conferences before, but the day after Julia Gillard announced a royal commission into the institutional abuse of children George Pell was falling apart in front of the cameras.

He had suffered a mighty defeat. For twenty years, in the face of growing public anger about paedophile priests, political leaders had backed the Catholic Church. Despite protests from victims, their parents, Anglican bishops, lawyers, academics, child protection advocates, a number of Catholic priests, newspapers and police, the business of cleaning up the mess of child abuse had been left to the churches themselves. When Pell provoked an outcry by walking the paedophile Gerald Ridsdale into court in 1993, Jeff Kennett hosed down calls for a royal commission. When Pell was accused himself of abusing boys, John Howard blocked calls for a royal commission. When the former archbishop of Brisbane, Peter Hollingworth, was forced to resign as governor-general – his fall provoked by his muddled response to paedophilia in Anglican ranks – his own church called for a national inquiry. Howard again refused. Pell concurred: "It is not at all clear to me that we need a royal commission." He never saw the need for the state to investigate the churches, particularly his own. When a nine-year inquiry uncovered the rot in the church in Ireland, Pell was on hand to claim nothing like it was needed here. "Ireland is not Australia."

But after Ireland the political protection offered the churches in Australia began to falter. How such old understandings, taken for granted for so long, begin to break down is all but impossible to track. A few cracks appear, a floor sags, and then one day the whole house collapses. The appalling record of the church in Ireland entered the local imagination. This was not Belgium or Spain but the mother country of Australian Catholicism. The crimes were not all in the past and their concealment was contemporary. In July 2011, a week after the publication of a report on the church in Cork, the Irish prime minister, Enda Kenny, delivered a blast heard around the world:

> The revelations of the Cloyne Report have brought the Government, Irish Catholics and the Vatican to an unprecedented juncture … because for the first time in Ireland, a report into child sexual-abuse exposes an attempt by the Holy See to frustrate an Inquiry in a sovereign, democratic republic as little as three years ago, not three decades ago. And in doing so, the Cloyne Report excavates

the dysfunction, disconnection, elitism, the narcissism that dominate the culture of the Vatican to this day. The rape and torture of children were downplayed or "managed" to uphold, instead, the primacy of the institution, its power, standing and "reputation."

Seven months later, the premier of Victoria, Ted Baillieu, received a report on protecting vulnerable children by the retired Supreme Court judge Philip Cummins. He had not been asked to investigate the role of the churches but suggested it was time someone did: "There is a strong public interest in the ascertainment of whether past abuses have been institutionally hidden, whether religious organisations have been active or complicit in that suppression, and in revealing what processes and procedures were employed." Six weeks later, the pressure on the Baillieu government to hold an inquiry became irresistible when the *Age* published a confidential police report accusing the Catholic Church of protecting paedophiles and showing little sympathy for their victims. Victoria Police linked forty suicides in the state to abuse by half a dozen priests and brothers alone. Detective Sergeant Kevin Carson wrote: "It would appear that an investigation would uncover many more deaths as a consequence of clergy sexual abuse."

Baillieu was moderately brave. He announced not a royal commission but a parliamentary Inquiry into the Handling of Child Abuse by Religious and Other Organisations. Pell said he was willing to appear. As the inquiry was about to begin public hearings in October last year, Victoria Police accused the Melbourne archdiocese of the Catholic Church of hindering investigations, protecting priests, silencing victims and failing to "proactively seek out" offenders. They also attacked the process Pell had put in place in Melbourne in the 1990s to inquire into abuse and compensate victims:

> Victoria Police has serious concerns regarding the terms of this inquiry process and its appearance as a de facto substitute for criminal justice. As noted on its website, the Melbourne Response has

made a number of ex gratia payments to victims. In spite of this, it has not referred a single complaint to Victoria Police.

This was damaging. That police in Victoria were no longer willing to protect the church – as they had, vigorously, for a very long time – was a key to the breakdown of old understandings across Australia that the Catholic Church could be left to look after its own. Pell was affronted by this *volte-face*. He shrugged off calls for his resignation. Then a disgruntled detective chief inspector from Newcastle, Peter Fox, turned on the church in New South Wales. On 8 November last year he published an open letter to the premier, Barry O'Farrell:

> I have investigated so many sexual assaults in my thirty-five years of policing I've lost count. Having spent most of those years at the coal face I have seen the worst society can dredge up, particularly the evil of paedophilia within the Catholic Church …
>
> I can testify from my own experience that the church covers up, silences victims, hinders police investigations, alerts offenders, destroys evidence and moves priests to protect the good name of the church. None of that stops at the Victorian border … the whole system needs to be exposed; the clergy covering up these crimes must to be brought to justice and the network protecting paedophile priests dismantled. There should be no place for evil or its guardians to hide.

When O'Farrell announced a modest inquiry into police work in the Newcastle region, there were frustrated cries from all sides for a royal commission. Pell counter-attacked, first in a feisty interview he gave the *Australian* and then next day in his weekly column in Sydney's *Sunday Telegraph*. That morning in St Mary's Cathedral he preached against royal commissions, and on the steps afterwards he told the press such things weren't needed to bring justice to victims. Hadn't the church apologised and set up procedures for redress? "I think it needs to be demonstrated that there is maladministration and corruption on a wide scale before there is any general royal commission."

Julia Gillard was with world leaders in Bali the day Fox published his letter. The prime minister told a press conference at Nusa Dua she was concerned and might have something more to say about it when she got home. On her return a couple of days later there was "an avalanche of calls from Labor backbenchers and independent MPs for a commission," reported Phillip Coorey in the *Sydney Morning Herald*. Malcolm Fraser and the independent MPs Tony Windsor and Nick Xenophon were among the people urging an inquiry. This was the Sunday of Pell's frantic counter-attack. Gillard talked to her senior colleagues next morning. "There was no resistance," wrote Coorey. "Everyone was in furious agreement." Gillard planned to make the announcement once cabinet met that afternoon.

Pell had spoken to Tony Abbott. What passed between the leader of the Opposition and his spiritual adviser is not known but Abbott would not mount a last-ditch stand on behalf of the church. About 3.30 p.m. he put out an eloquent statement:

> Wherever abuse has occurred it must be tackled and it must be tackled vigorously, openly and transparently. It's clear that for a long period there was insufficient awareness and insufficient vigilance when it came to predatory behaviour by people in positions of authority over children. A lot of terrible things have been done, and a lot of people have suffered deeply.
>
> For these reasons, if the government were to propose a royal commission to investigate the sexual abuse of children, it is something the Coalition would be prepared to support.

Half an hour later, Gillard took her plan to cabinet. There was no dissent. She called Pell. "She said this wasn't an anti-Catholic move but more general and I said I acknowledged that. I said I wasn't surprised that it wasn't anti-Catholic and I was grateful." The press conference she called at 5.40 p.m. was perilously late for television news crews. She began: "I will be recommending to the governor-general the establishment of a royal commission into institutional responses to instances and allegations of child sexual abuse in Australia."

The cardinal was beaten. Next day, 13 November 2012, he called the press to Polding House, the headquarters of the church in Sydney. Everyone in that room knew this was a remarkable occasion. Pell wore on his dark suit insignia of both church and state: a cross and the gold pin of a Companion of the Order of Australia. An incongruous kiss-curl fell on his forehead. He was pale and fleshy. On the ring finger of his right hand he wore a heavy sheath of gold. Once he had settled and the cameras were running, he began to read from a typed sheet of paper. What had to be done had to be done. In the louche talk of the press and the police, it's called eating a shit sandwich:

> The Catholic bishops of Australia have welcomed the royal commission, which was announced by the prime minister last night. We think it's an opportunity to help the victims; it's an opportunity to clear the air, to separate fact from fiction. The first thing I would like to do is to repeat what I and the church leadership have said for the last sixteen years, which is that we are not interested in denying the extent of misdoing in the Catholic Church. We object to it being exaggerated; we object to being described as the only cab on the rank; we acknowledge, with shame, the extent of the problem and I want to assure you that we have been serious in attempting to eradicate it and deal with it and one of the reasons why we welcome the royal commission is that this commission will enable those claims to be validated or found to be a significant exaggeration. Obviously we shall cooperate with the royal commission, we'll cooperate fully.

Under questioning, the carefully crafted good work of his opening rhetoric fell apart. The cardinal was unrepentant. He was there to defend his patch. The real victim in all this was the Catholic Church and its enemy was the press.

There is a persistent press campaign against the Catholic Church's adequacies and inadequacies in this area that does not necessarily represent the percentage of the problem that we offer. In other words because there's a press campaign focused largely on us it does not mean that we are largely the principal culprit ...

I certainly very much regret the general smearing [that] "The church is covering up, the church has done nothing." Because that's not the case, it's demonstrably not the case.

Pell had a point about the media: very little of this scandal would have emerged but for newspaper and television investigations. Over thirty years, beginning with scattered reports of apparently isolated outrages, paedophile abuse and its cover-up by the religious had become one of the biggest stories in the world. But Pell had long thought it was time for the media to abandon the issue – in the interests of the victims themselves.

One question I think that might be asked is just to what extent the victims are *helped* by the continuing furore in the press over these allegations. The pursuit of justice is an absolute entitlement for everyone. That being said, to what extent are wounds simply opened by the rerunning of events which have been reported not only once but many times previously?

His detachment was astonishing. So was the undercurrent of anger as reporters grilled him about his own record of dealing with paedophilia in Catholic ranks. For the most part he was lofty and cool but once or twice under fire showed real passion. "The seal of the confessional is inviolable," he said, rolling the word on his tongue. "Inviolable."

Pell had done himself great harm. He couldn't help it. As a man of the church he fought back when the church came under fire. The impact on television that night was terrible. Catholics were appalled. Old political allies distanced themselves. O'Farrell told his parliament: "I struggle to understand why, if a priest confesses to another priest that he has been involved with paedophile activities, that that information should not be brought to the notice of police." Next day in Brisbane, quizzed about the secrecy of the confessional, Tony Abbott said: "Everyone has to obey the law, regardless of what job they're doing, regardless of what position they hold." And did that include priests? "Indeed."

Pell's faith that he had the public onside proved a delusion. The Fairfax/Nielsen poll was in the field in the nights following publication of the Fox letter. In all his years as a pollster Nielsen director John Stirton has never seen such a result: 95 per cent support for a royal commission. Somewhere along the line, perhaps a long time ago, Pell and his church lost the support of the people. The politicians were merely catching up. On the night she was toppled by Kevin Rudd, Gillard listed the commission among the many achievements of her embattled government. Extravagant claims were never her bag. But as she was leaving her last press conference, she allowed herself a big prediction: "This royal commission is now working its way around the country. I believe it will have many years of work in front of it. But it will change the nation."

PRIEST

The presbytery of St Alipius is a redbrick gothic bungalow built when gold money was still washing through Ballarat. It sits in a Catholic compound of brick and granite schools and convents where the road from Melbourne reaches town. White crosses stand on the gables of the house as if to ward off evil from all points of the compass. The plan, if that was indeed the plan, failed spectacularly. When young Father George Pell moved his things into the presbytery in 1973, that corner of Ballarat was one of the most dangerous places in Australia for children. Already living in the presbytery was Father Gerald Ridsdale, chaplain at the little primary school standing on the other side of the church. He was raping the children. All four members of the staff, all Christian Brothers, were abusing the children in the school. They would not be exposed for twenty years. George Pell, back from his studies in Rome and Oxford, noticed nothing.

Ballarat was his town. His parents owned the Royal Oak. George Sr was huge, down-to-earth and Protestant. Lil was fierce, gentle and made all the decisions that mattered in her son's life. She was devoted to the Catholic Church. A portrait of old Daniel Mannix, archbishop of Melbourne since 1917, hung in her kitchen. Her son would one day write: "She was a woman of great strength and faith: a faith I suspect that was very Irish, and probably in particular a faith typical of the west of Ireland in its certainties and in its impatience with theological subtleties." The pub was working-class but not rough. George Sr ran an SP bookmaking operation out of the front bar and hid the books under his children's beds. He enforced the rules. Children brought up in a pub learn to tolerate all sorts and to value rules. Once they were teenagers, young George and his sister Margaret helped out in the bar in the school holidays but their mother was preparing her children for a life that would take them a long way from the Royal Oak.

Though raised Catholic from birth – tribal Catholic in a town where priests, nuns and brothers ruled the Catholic roost – Lil's big, confident boy had a conversion in adolescence that determined the course of his spiritual life and the trajectory of his career. At the age of fourteen he fell under the spell of B.A. Santamaria:

> As a teenager, probably in 1955, I first heard him talk to a packed cathedral hall in Ballarat on the menace of communism. He set out to identify the mighty forces under the swirl of events. He often appealed to history. We felt we too belonged to the forces of good fighting the new faces of evil, as saints and heroes had done for thousands of years. He placed us in a grand tradition of worthy struggle and combat, where we felt we could do our bit. Some of us never completely lost this conviction.

It was the time of the great Labor Split, the height of the Cold War. Santamaria was at his most mesmerising as he recruited young warriors for the Movement to defend the bulwark of civilisation, the Catholic Church. Communism seemed the enemy when Pell was a boy. Later, when that curse was defeated, it transpired that something just as sinister lay behind its mask: secular liberalism, which had been allowed to take root not only in the world, but in the church. Others might see nothing particularly troubling in the swirl of events, but Santamaria instilled in his followers a habit of discovering everywhere in the world around them a contest between the forces of good and evil.

The boy was "reasonably bright" according to the historian John Molony, who was one of his teachers at St Patrick's, Ballarat. "Unquestionably an unusual human being. Enormously talented in sport. He was a leader, president of every possible organisation in the college." He was big and used his size to get his way. He debated and acted. The grand Pooh-Bah in *The Mikado* was a role he played more than once in his early years. He ran, rowed and played football with such skill that Richmond offered him a contract in his final year. He signed but had other ideas. St Patrick's was a great recruiting ground for the priesthood. Pell had shown a religiosity — saying the rosary in the back of the car on the way to football — that was not out of place in the school. Nor was the ambition to have a priest in the family surprising in the pub trade or the Irish tribe from which his mother sprang. Pell says he fought his calling for a long time: "I feared and suspected and eventually became convinced that God wanted me to do His work, and I was never able to successfully escape that conviction." His biographer, Tess Livingstone, noted that "no serious romances" had developed after school dances. Perhaps the sight of Mannix at the age of ninety-five being given a great ovation in Ballarat may have helped the boy make up his mind. Pell's calling seemed always linked to the possibilities of high office. In late 1959 he told his parents he was going to be a priest. His father was hostile. His mother was overjoyed.

So many young men were training for the priesthood that Werribee Park had burst at the seams. These were years of triumphalist high confidence in the mission of the church. Pell found himself among 115 young men living, studying and praying at the direction of the Jesuits in the Italianate pile that housed Corpus Christi College. The place was demanding and inflexible. The saying at Werribee was: "You keep the rules and the rules will keep you." Pell thrived. He liked this life and Werribee has remained, ever since, his model for the proper training of young men for the priesthood. Roughhouse antics were not unknown. Sport and amateur theatricals were part of the program. But Werribee demanded prayer, lots of prayer. Pell's superiors admired the young man's forthright ways and eagerness for responsibility. In his third year he was put in charge of the discipline of new arrivals. There were those among the underlings who found him harsh, formal and unforgiving. Pell's reputation as a bully dates back to Werribee. But those closer to him remember more vividly how certain he was of his faith. He never criticised. He never doubted. "He is a guy for whom it has always been very clear," recalled Brian Scarlett some forty years after their time together in the seminary. "He was exactly the same as he is now."

Every summer Werribee students went over to Phillip Island to supervise a camp for altar boys. For a couple of summers Pell was helping to organise the fun, games and worship at Smiths Beach. He seems to have been liked and popular. But one of the altar boys, Phillip Scott, would later claim to have disturbing memories of a seminarian he knew back then as Big George fondling his genitals:

> He would grab my hand when he could and would put my hand down his trousers. This would happen at play, in the water and on any occasion that it was possible. He was very skilful at grabbing me and forcing his hand down or grabbing my hand and forcing it down his pants. Especially when we were in our tents, Big George would come into the tents and start wrestling and having pillow fights and would grab me and thrust his hand down my pyjama pants.

Scott was about eleven. Years later he would say he saw a friend, Michael Foley, telling Big George to "fuck off" when he tried to molest him in the same way. He remembered Foley telling him he couldn't stand the abuse in the camp and was going to burn the place down. Together they set a grass fire but the Country Fire Authority came and the camp survived. Scott embarked on a life of crime. About fifteen years after this summer he told his wife he had been molested when he was a little boy on Phillip Island by "a big bastard called George." According to Scott, it was another fifteen years before he realised who the seminarian was. Watching television one night in about May 2000, he saw a man in episcopal purple he thought had "the same face and the same loping walk" as Big George. Pell was archbishop of Sydney before any of this surfaced. "The allegations against me are lies," he declared. "I deny them totally and utterly." Scott replied: "I will stand by what I said till the day I die." A retired judge, hired by the church to investigate the matter, found Scott "gave the impression that he was speaking honestly from an actual recollection" but in the end he was "not satisfied" his complaint was established. Both sides claimed victory.

Sir James O'Collins, the bishop of Ballarat, had his eye on young Pell. O'Collins had been bishop since World War II, was a close friend of

Santamaria's and had been a leader of the Movement from its early days. Santamaria valued the bishop not least because he had once been an active member of the Plumbers Union. O'Collins was a straightforward man who loved the life of bishop. Seeing in Pell the makings of a champion, he was the young man's first patron. Pell called him: "father and friend to me, [he] sponsored my progress and offered me marvellous educational opportunities." In 1963 he plucked Pell out of Werribee and sent him to study at Propaganda Fide in Rome.

Vatican II was underway. Pell, swept up in the hopes and drama of the Council, counted himself in those days as "deeply committed to its liberal reforms." His Italian was soon serviceable. He loved the city; its pomp and its history. From this point, Rome would be his other country. He would always have a life there. In December 1966 he was ordained at St Peter's – his father stayed home to look after the pub – and the following year he presented a rather edgy dissertation defending the theology of Teilhard de Chardin for which he was granted high honours. After a summer working in a wealthy Baltimore parish, he arrived at Oxford. This was all part of O'Collins' plan: he wanted a formidable intellectual who could come home and take on the Catholic academics who continued to oppose the Movement.

Oxford changed Pell. It's an old story: he was seduced by English ways and English high culture. Oxford buffed and polished the boy from Ballarat. He came to see his years in the university town as at least as formative as his time in Rome. For the only time in his life he wondered if there was a God. "I came to understand the intellectual force of alternative views, of agnosticism," he told Luke Slattery of the *Australian*. Pell was not living in secular Oxford but at the Jesuits' Campion Hall, where he spent four years writing a thesis on the struggles of the primitive church against heresy. *The Exercise of Authority in Early Christianity from about 170 to about 270* earned Pell a doctorate and marked him for life not as a theologian, but a historian of the church. He knows theology, of course, but he brought to the controversies of his career the conviction that the beliefs and practices of the church were right because they were old. He was derided by his critics for this, but he came to see the church as essentially untouched by time.

No one could know this then, but the decade Pell spent in Werribee, Rome and Oxford marked a high tide for Catholicism in the modern West. At the age of thirty, with remarkable qualifications and great things expected of him, Pell was returning to Australia to work as a priest just as Catholics began to desert their church. He was a kid seminarian when the Pill hit the market. He had his head in the turmoil of the third-century church when Paul VI reaffirmed Rome's absolute opposition to contraception. *Humanae Vitae* brought rebellion to the pews. Attendance at mass began to fall away. Those who stayed did what Vatican II had said they could: decide the matter according to their own consciences. In the struggle with pleasure inside the Catholic Church that began with Paul's encyclical in 1968, dogma lost. Pell's liberal spring was soon over. He joined the pessimists like Santamaria who feared for the church if "the principle of the moral autonomy of the individual" was allowed to override the authority of the pope. "Within fifteen years," wrote Santamaria, "the forces unleashed by that principle had eroded the foundations of Catholicism throughout the Western world."

Dr Pell set himself against conscience and for authority. Rarely from this time would he preach or write without taking a swipe at conscience and reminding Catholics of their obligations of obedience. It would win him few friends, many enemies and high office.

*

Swan Hill in the flatlands of the Murray was a trial he knew he could endure. The church had not invested in his education to employ him forever as a parish priest on the outskirts of the diocese of Ballarat. But nothing in his training had prepared Pell for what was lying in wait when he returned from Europe. He would claim not even to have been aware of paedophile priests and brothers around him in the diocese. He would be down in Melbourne fifteen years later before he saw it as his duty to face the issue. At Swan Hill in 1971, the young man resigned himself with good humour to a stint as a curate in a remote country town.

Ballarat had a new bishop, Ronald Mulkearns, remembered unhappily by Mildura detective Denis Ryan as "an exacting man, aloof and authoritative, who spoke with a studied deliberation, as if his words carried more gravity than that of a mere mortal." Mulkearns was protecting the paedophile priests of the diocese just as O'Collins had done. When parishioners complained or police threatened, the priest was sent to rehab or straight to another parish. There were so many abusive priests in the western half of Victoria in these years that the diocese would one day be seen as bad even by the worst standards of the church. But here, as elsewhere in the Catholic world, to denounce paedophile priests to the police was not considered pastoral. After all, forgiveness is the fundamental business of the church. Nor did turning them over to the authorities accord with the ancient understanding of the church that it was somehow not subject to the laws of the world. Rome had its own laws, its own courts and its own punishments. Priests were seen by the Catholic community – politicians, lawyers and police – to be protected by a kind of diplomatic immunity. For years, Ballarat's most notorious paedophile priests, Monsignor John Day and Father Gerard Ridsdale, continued to assault children with the knowledge of both church and police. Detective Ryan, who lost his job trying to stop Day, wrote:

> Like O'Collins, Mulkearns was just following orders. The Nuremberg defence. If a priest was raping kids, it reflected poorly on the church, all the way up to the Vatican. Move the priest on and consign the victims to earthly oblivion. If the police intervened, stare them down. If one copper could not be stared down, the Catholic Mafia within the police force would come to the rescue. It was a perfect situation. Flawless. And it had been going on for decades.

The church has always had to forgive its priests. They are sacred persons, "another Christ" according to Catholic teaching, but in the experience of an ancient institution they are also fallible human beings doing a hard job. "Most of it is a pretty tough life, hard and cold," says Neil Ormerod, professor of theology at the Australian Catholic University. "While there are many good men out there, there are also a lot of very dysfunctional guys, not necessarily sexually dysfunctional but alcoholic or with few personal skills or into power. But they have to have men in parishes no matter how dysfunctional they may be. The alternative is, really, that they close up shop." So the question facing the church has always been: what can't be forgiven? The answer appears to be very little by way of sexual misbehaviour so long as it does not embarrass the church. In 1962 Rome issued *Crimen sollicitationis*, a highly secret direction to the bishops of the world to keep under wraps investigation of priests for a few particularly grim crimes: soliciting sex in the confessional, having sex with animals, sex with each other and sex with children. These were not unforgivable. They didn't require priests to be turned over to the police. They were just so shameful they had to be kept secret.

But the secrecy was breaking down. Monsignor Day suddenly told his flock in January 1972 that he was moving on. A few days later, Melbourne's scandal sheet *Truth* claimed police were protecting an unnamed paedophile priest in a country town in Victoria. A member of parliament – a former policeman – named Day in the Legislative Assembly and called for an inquiry into his being allowed to go to Portugal for therapy. Months later a full account of the priest's crimes, including details from twelve of his victims, was published in the *Melbourne Observer*. No charges were laid but no priest in the Ballarat diocese could be oblivious to the scandal. Later that year Mulkearns sent Day to a fresh parish, tiny little Timboon down by the coast. He died there in 1978.

Looking back to that time, Pell does not believe the church should be judged harshly. He acknowledges there was "a fear of scandal" that led to cover-ups, but told the Victorian inquiry this year, "Many in the church did not understand just what damage was being done to the victims." But surely it was understood that these were crimes that carried serious prison terms? "With due deference," Pell replied, "I take you back to the 1970s. It was only in the 1970s that articles started to appear about the significance and importance and the terrible crimes of paedophilia. This crime, I suppose – what was it? The sodomy of children. That was always regarded as being totally reprehensible." But not so reprehensible that priests at that time should be handed over to police or expelled from the church. Once again, Pell saw the church protected by its own ignorance. Last year he told the *Australian*: "Back in those days, they were entitled to think of paedophilia as simply a sin that you would repent of. They didn't realise that in the worst cases it was an addiction, a raging addiction."

Whether the new curate at Swan Hill paid much attention to the Day scandal that broke in his first year back home isn't known. People who met him then remember a keen young man with hair almost down to his collar who was given a bit of a hard time for his Oxford ways and got on well with kids. "He loved swimming in the local pool with the youngsters," one of his parishioners told Tess Livingstone. "He loved kicking around a football with the boys. And he loved food." The commentator Ronald Conway met Pell at this time: "I was struck by his sense of humour and clever mimicry, the subtle blend of English fluency and Roman poise, all of which could easily erupt into the Aussie earthiness of a Ballarat boy and hotelier's son who had been around."

After two years out on the river, Mulkearns brought Pell to town and moved him into the St Alipius presbytery with Ridsdale and two other priests. Pell says he saw nothing that hinted at Ridsdale's pursuit of children: "He concealed his crimes from me and other priests in Ballarat, from parishioners and from his own family." While Pell had a full slate of duties as curate – daily mass at a girls' school and weekly mass at the parish church – Mulkearns was grooming him for what was, perhaps, his real calling: education. After Pell had served a few months as chaplain and part-time lecturer at Ballarat's little Catholic teachers' college, the bishop appointed him episcopal vicar for education. His job description remains rather vague. He denies responsibility for the hell of abuse at St Alipius

Primary. "I wasn't the executive running education," he told 60 Minutes. "I don't want to pretend that those things were always handled well, but it wasn't my bag. I was responsible for one area of church life and I fulfilled my responsibilities. In the areas where I didn't have responsibilities, I wasn't obliged to act."

Ridsdale, the headmaster, Brother Robert Best, and Christian Brothers Ted Dowlan and Stephen Frances Farrell were all later convicted of crimes against the children of St Alipius. They worked together. "Ridsdale and Best would hand around the children," one of their victims, Robert Walsh, told the Melbourne Herald Sun years later. "They had me in the bedroom, in the garage and even inside the church." Some of the boys found the courage to speak out. One who complained to Best was given to Ridsdale to rape. In that particularly devout diocese children were not believed when they tried to talk of what was being done to them. Many would later commit suicide. The police who spurred Ted Baillieu into action linked thirty-four suicides to Best and Ridsdale. Detective Sergeant Kevin Carson wrote: "While speaking to victims who had been abused by Ridsdale and Best, it was apparent the majority of suicides were committed subsequent to abuse having occurred at St Alipius, Ballarat East."

Someone must have had wind of these crimes because in 1974 the paedophile ring was broken up. Ridsdale was sent to a "national pastoral institute" for therapy and then given a fresh parish. Best re-emerged from the same institute to teach at Christian Brothers' schools over the next twenty years in Box Hill, Geelong and Warrnambool. When the police caught up with him, his order spent a fortune defending him at a number of trials that dragged on for over a decade before he was jailed for fourteen years on dozens of counts of indecent assault going all the way back to St Alipius. Brother Dowlan was first sent to St Thomas More College in Forest Hill – where he was swiftly caught abusing boys – and then brought back to Ballarat to be a boarding master at St Patrick's.

Dowlan was an aggressive but rather pathetic little man who hung around showers staring at naked children. He ran young athletes into the ground, then massaged their thighs. He took boys to the back of the class-room to feel them up behind the coats hanging there. One, Tim Green, rebuffed him: "I said, 'This is not fair, I can't fight back,' and he stopped. There were forty-five kids in that class and he must have tried everyone." Green was sure the staff at St Patrick's knew about Dowlan. He told me: "All the boys talked about what was going on. I was only twelve years old and it was as plain as the nose on my face. How adults couldn't figure it out was beyond me."

One afternoon in 1974, in the changing sheds of the town's Eureka Stock-ade swimming pool, Green was talking to a few schoolfriends when Pell appeared and began to change into his bathers. Green had seen Pell often around the school and thought him a big figure at St Patrick's. To this day he wonders where he found the courage to talk to the priest as he did. He remembers a brief exchange: "I said, 'You should really do something about what's going on at St Pat's.' He asked, 'What do you mean?' I said, 'Brother Dowlan is touching up the little boys.' Pell replied, 'Don't be ridiculous,' and walked out." Green is now putting his name to this episode. When the *Age* ran an account that did not name him in 2002, Pell replied: "At a distance of twenty-eight years, I have no recollection of any such conversation. If I was approached and thought the stories plausible, I would have informed the Christian Brothers. I do not remember hearing rumours about Dowlan at that stage, a man I hardly knew." At the end of that year Dowlan left Bal-larat and there followed a series of brief postings over twenty years to schools and orphanages. Eventually he faced sixty-four charges and, after a plea bargain with the crown, pleaded guilty to sixteen that included the abuse of two boys at St Alipius and four at St Patrick's.

Pell was a born administrator and a skilled empire-builder with a talent for extracting money from governments. With the supply of nuns and brothers drying up, the church had great plans to expand its teachers' col-leges in Victoria. Pell became headmaster of the renamed Aquinas College in Ballarat, one of four that rebadged themselves as the Institute of Catho-lic Education, and began a long and ultimately successful campaign for academic recognition and federal funding. Pell would prove himself extraordinarily adept at sectarian lobbying. By 1980 he was running all four campuses of the institute. He taught but he was not much of a teacher. Exchange of ideas was not his strength. He expected everyone around him, staff and students, to be frank. He wanted to know what people thought. He despised the wishy-washy. He proclaimed: to maintain standards there must be failures. He was not two-faced: if he said he would back you, he backed you. You always knew where he stood. He was rarely surprising. He had a useful reputation for getting his way.

The vice-chancellor of the institute was Father Eric D'Arcy, an urbane, highly intelligent priest Pell had befriended at Oxford. They met at a performance of *Othello* at Stratford-upon-Avon and the bond between them was key to Pell's career. D'Arcy was chaplain to the Movement. He was the philosophical mind in clerical garb that accompanied Santamaria all the way. He became senior lecturer in philosophy at Melbourne University and later a bishop. He would be in both Australia and Rome a superbly connected advocate for Pell. This was also the time Pell drew close to that other Movement leader, Sir James O'Collins, now ancient and living in the old bishop's palace in Ballarat. Pell moved in for the last couple of years of O'Collins' life. It was a good time. They lived well. When the old man died in 1983, Pell was sent to administer the outlying parish of Bungaree, from which address he was rescued the following year by being named rector of Corpus Christi College.

His old seminary had fallen on lean times. Vocations were way down. The mansion in Werribee had been abandoned in favour of a modest college at Clayton in the suburbs of Melbourne. Pell didn't hesitate: he would restore the routines he had loved when he began his own training. Going back to the past was always and instinctively his prescription for renewal. In the face of general hostility from the seminarians, he introduced "a few small changes": more prayer, more decades of the rosary, daily mass and an end to questioning of papal teaching, particularly on contraception. "The majority of the staff and a goodly percentage of the students felt that

I was heading in the wrong direction," he told Tess Livingstone. There were sixty-three men when he arrived and numbers continued to dwindle. But fighting the good fight for orthodoxy at Corpus Christi drew him closer to Santamaria and impressed Rome. There was a new pope, Józef Wojtyła, with huge ambitions to restore the authority of the church and confront the decadence of the West. He believed the proper training of priests was fundamental to this mission. John Paul II was the right pope for George Pell. It seems that on his visit to Melbourne in 1986, the pontiff was persuaded to make him one of Melbourne's three auxiliary bishops. The news came as an uncomfortable surprise to the city's archbishop, Sir Frank Little, who made it plain he had not asked for Pell: "Others do the choosing."

On 21 May 1987, twenty-eight bishops and 300 priests gathered in St Patrick's Cathedral for Pell's consecration. Pell attested to the strength of his faith and the depths of his obedience to the pope. Choirs sang Vaughan Williams and Elgar. Clouds of incense drifted over the crowd. The two-hour show had, according to the *Age*, "enough pomp and ceremony to satisfy the most old-fashioned Roman Catholic." After lying for a time prostrate before the altar, Pell knelt in front of Little, who handed him a mitre, ring and staff to mark his entry into "the high priesthood of Christ." Pell's seat was Mentone, a suburb on Port Phillip Bay, but his duties were far from clear. He was on a leash. Little was his boss. He couldn't build. He couldn't make changes. He told friends: "It's a bit boring because no one wants to pick a fight with you."

The fight that mattered was happening in America. As Pell was installed in Melbourne, juries in Louisiana were awarding millions to the victims of a paedophile priest, Gilbert Gauthe. The victims' lawyers were angry Catholics. "We didn't want to begin and end with Gauthe," said Raul Bencomo. "We wanted to get to the upper councils of the church to say, 'You're not running a good clean house.'" The children abused by this one priest in one corner of one state would cost the church in America more than $20 million. Lawyers and priests assisting the victims prepared a report on abuse by clergy and sent a copy to every bishop in America with a warning that unless the priests were stopped and the victims given help, the church might be facing a bill of a billion dollars by the end of the decade. The bishops stalled. Sex abuse by Catholic priests began to be reported around the world as an American story, but the church everywhere saw problems looming.

In 1988 the Australian bishops set up a Special Issues committee. The Orwellian name covered its unhappy purpose: to draft a protocol to protect the church from victims of abuse. The man overseeing the committee was Mulkearns of Ballarat. While the bishops dithered over the draft, the church in Australia took out insurance against victims' claims. A list was drawn up of known paedophile priests and brothers still working in parishes and schools who were too risky to cover. The finished protocol of 1992, marked "Strictly confidential. For bishops, major superiors and superiors only," essentially served the purposes of the insurers. Victims were offered little more than compassionate rhetoric while the needs of accused priests were set out in detail: they were to be given lawyers, "such spiritual and psychological assistance as he may require" and the personal, supportive attention of their bishop. No admissions were to be made to victims or to anyone else "that the accused is guilty, that there is any liability in damages, that any particular course of action will follow any investigations." The only punishments facing priests were removal from children and a course of "psychological therapy." Throwing them out of the church wasn't canvassed in the document. There was no obligation to report the crimes of paedophile priests to the police. Bishops were warned not to "obstruct or pervert the process of justice" but, however grave the allegations, to deal with them in-house. And great care was to be taken dealing with the media: "The minimisation of scandal, as well as the reputation of all involved, should be taken into account." The protocol was not to be made public. This was secret church business.

Pell voted for the 1992 protocol but otherwise took no part in the bishops' deliberations. Nor does he seem to have had a word to say about clerical paedophilia as the issue began, slowly at first, to become a matter of general discussion. A request to his office for anything Pell said on this subject in the years he was an auxiliary bishop of Melbourne yielded nothing. Yet he was a busy polemicist. In Ballarat he had edited the diocesan magazine *The Light*. In Melbourne he wrote for newspapers and the new magazine *AD 2000*. His subject was the church and its need for renewal, not by facing terrible failings as they came to light, but by rediscovering Catholic truth and reviving obedience to John Paul II.

AD 2000 was Bob Santamaria's last great effort to save the Catholic Church. He saw the magazine rallying Catholics to "an active, resolute, prayerful and intelligent fight" against the forces of liberalism. He was full of dread. As usual, there was no time to lose: the church faced its greatest threat since the Pelagians of the fifth century queried original sin. So he began *AD 2000* "not merely as a matter of duty to defend the faith but as a matter of necessity to prevent the total destruction of the base from which it draws its numbers and resources." Pell's youthful face appeared often in the pages of *AD 2000*. So too did other Santamaria favourites like Greg Sheridan and Frank Devine, but Pell gave the magazine clout. He was a bishop. And the real targets of the magazine were the liberal bishops of Australia – which was nearly all of them. The magazine applauded celibacy and raged against birth control, abortion and homosexuality. It belittled critics who claimed the church had a problem on its hands with paedophile priests. The magazine ran letters accusing victims' groups of showing "a spirit of hatred and vindictiveness that knows few limits." Devine condemned the ABC for "enjoying a real wallow" in this "fashionable" subject and ridiculed the notion that any Catholic, let alone the pope, should apologise "for the atrocious behaviour of a few priests." The readers of *AD 2000* were assured that the real crisis facing the church was not "the widely publicised cases of clerical paedophilia" but "the influence of progressivist priests" undermining Catholic doctrine and the authority of Rome.

Meanwhile, priests in Pell's bailiwick were abusing children. The zone of his responsibilities extended from the Mornington Peninsula up to the Dandenongs. In those suburbs were at least three parishes with paedophile priests: Doveton, Oakleigh and Gardenvale. Pell reassured the Victorian inquiry this year that the oversight of auxiliary bishops ensures priests now follow the rules. "Auxiliary bishops are responsible for a particular area – I think there are three zones in Melbourne – and they certainly would monitor what is happening there." Yet he told the inquiry that back in his day he hadn't known about the paedophile priests of Melbourne. "As an auxiliary bishop to Archbishop Little I did not have the authority to handle these matters and had only some general impressions about the response that was being made at the time." However, he would appear to have been in a position to know a good deal because he sat on the Curia of Bishops with Little, the two other auxiliaries and the vicar-general who handled the growing number of complaints against priests in the archdiocese. Even so, Pell insists he was more or less in the dark all through these years and that Little never confided in him. "He never raised the issue with me personally ... for some strange reason he never spoke to anybody about it." But when Little faced fresh trouble in Doveton he sent Pell to sort things out.

*

Doveton was a raw housing commission suburb built for migrants working at International Harvester, General Motors-Holden and Heinz. The people of Doveton were largely English in the early days but by the 1980s they had been joined by Indians, Sri Lankans and South Americans. These poor, faithful Catholics sent their children to Holy Family Primary School and into the clutches of Father Peter Searson. The church had sent a succession of terrible priests to Doveton – some violent, many paedophiles – before Searson took up his duties in 1984. A former teacher at the school, Carmel Rafferty, told the Victorian inquiry:

> I suppose the archdiocesan people who do the placing figured out it was a community of people who would not wake up too quickly if they had a problem priest in their midst ... a community of people who would be, as all of us were, brought up to believe in obedience and loyalty – and the mystique and aura of the priesthood, which was paramount.

Searson was a bad man. Complaints about him had been pouring in for years to the Catholic Education Office, to the vicars-general of the diocese and to Archbishop Little. A delegation of teachers came to complain to Pell about Searson in 1989. A second delegation met him in 1991. But Searson was left to abuse children in Doveton for another six years.

The church had known about Searson for a long time. In the 1950s he was strapping the naked buttocks of boys at Marist Brothers' College, Mount Gambier. He left the Brothers to become a priest. A stint as a military chaplain in Europe may have explained his taste for combat fatigues and the delusion that he was a lieutenant colonel. He carried a revolver. In the early 1970s he was let loose on the blind and deaf community of Melbourne. At this time he groped a (sighted) woman who had come to him for religious instruction, explaining that that was how he gave sex instruction to the blind. His attacks continued when he became parish priest at Our Lady of Mount Carmel at Sunbury in the late 1970s. The police interviewed him in 1982 but the young girl he assaulted declined to lay charges. After this brush with the law, he promised the church not to take children either into the confessional or the presbytery. Father Phil O'Donnell, who joined him at Sunbury about this time, told the Victorian inquiry: "It was obvious – and unbelievably obvious – that Father Searson had a very serious personality disorder."

Little moved Searson to Doveton in 1984. The headmaster of Holy Family Primary, Graeme Sleeman, was shocked. He had been to see the archbishop several times to ask him to send a pastoral priest to this tough parish. Instead he got this man. "I was on a fishing trip and saw it in the *Advocate* and nearly had a heart attack." He told the Victorian inquiry: "When Searson was appointed, my phone rang hot with people telling me how bad he was, what he had done, what he had not done, in Sunbury." The new priest built a high wire fence around the school. He locked people in and locked them out. He was obsessed with making children go to confession again and again:

> Some of the children came to me and said, "Father's creepy. I don't like going to confession with him." Boys used to say to me, "I'm not keen to be an altar boy, Father's creepy." I think it was his second year there when they were all taken over to confession on a particular day and a young girl came out of the church screaming. I

found her and asked her what had happened and she informed me that Father had interfered with her. I went and got my 2IC, who was a female, and she spoke to her and then we notified the local educational consultant about what had taken place. There was to-ing and fro-ing and eventually the consultant informed me that he had spoken to Father and it was "all a blow-out; he's doing such a good job in the parish. People are out to get him."

The young girl, terribly disturbed, refused to go to the police and left for another school. When it was discovered that Searson had a fourteen-year-old Indian girl living alone with him in the presbytery, the Catholic Education Office merely counselled him. When Sleeman caught him stealing school funds, the office allowed the priest to pay the $40,000 back. Sleeman was profoundly disappointed: "I thought we had him on toast." Parents were complaining all the time. In 1986 a meeting of fifty parents and parishioners called for the priest to be removed. A petition of seventy names went to the archdiocese. Nothing was done. Sleeman threatened to resign. "I believed that by my staying at Doveton I was validating Searson's behaviour and condoning everything he did, and that was the furthest thing from the truth." The church stuck with the priest. The headmaster went.

Carmel Rafferty came to the school in 1987, about a year after Pell became auxiliary bishop. Even before she took the job, her local priest had warned her about Searson. "You don't really want to work for him, do you?" he asked. The staff at Holy Family warned her at once that he was not safe with children. They tried never to leave him alone with them. At their first meeting, Searson made her extremely uneasy by declaring the children were all masturbators. Soon after Rafferty began at the school, the Catholic Education Office asked the teachers to keep a record of incidents involving him. Rafferty was soon hearing complaints from teachers, parents, social workers, local police and children:

Children continued to report to teachers and beg for safety. Children came running inside to a teacher hysterical on two occasions when the priest was trying to single out a child and force the child into the presbytery to discuss why that child refused to serve on the altar. The same student mentioned earlier – normally a happy level-headed youngster who participated fully in school life – who became hysterical made a further disclosure in that condition of being made to go into the presbytery, where something inappropriate, which he described to me, had taken place sometime in the previous year, and he was traumatised by the prospect of a repeat.

Whatever Pell did behind the scenes, after the first delegation of teachers came to see him about Searson in 1989, the priest remained in the parish and at the school. The priest's behaviour grew more sinister. Rafferty told the inquiry:

In 1991 Searson was exhibiting violent desperation in his, what looked to me like, although I did not know the word then, grooming attempts. He then began frequenting the boys' toilets several times a day. It was the final straw, a big concern to us. The principal authorised the three years 5 and 6 teachers to make a deputation to the area bishop for the south-eastern area at the time, who was Bishop Pell, to advise him of the danger to children and the need to remove the priest.

Pell did not remove the priest. Most of the delegation's complaints he dismissed as no more than general information "that Searson was extremely difficult to deal with and disliked by parents, staff and children." That was not enough. Nor was the fact that the police conducted two inquiries into Searson at this time. "They were inconclusive," said Pell. "The Catholic Education Office got the lawyers Minter Ellison to evaluate what was done and whether it was done properly, and they were still unable to pin anything on the man." At some point Searson was asked to hand in his gun. Otherwise he earned only a tongue-lashing.

I was asked by Archbishop Little to speak with Searson and direct him to conduct himself more appropriately and scrupulously. I did so, and I recall that Searson rejected the allegations of wrongdoing and strongly denied that he had acted inappropriately. He made clear that he greatly resented my raising these concerns with him. It was an unpleasant conversation.

Rafferty was keen to leave Holy Family. Applications for other teaching positions proved unsuccessful. During this time, she heard from police that "the priest had used a knife to threaten a girl when she and a friend were putting up overheads in the church." The parents decided not to press charges but Rafferty believes both the Catholic Education Office and the vicar-general were informed of this latest outrage. Her health poor and feeling "bullied, isolated and traumatised," she resigned from the school in March 1993: "I never got a job in the system again, although I tried very, very hard."

*

Rome gave Pell a magnificent appointment. From 1990 the young bishop from Australia sat on the Congregation for the Doctrine of the Faith. Under John Paul and the prefect of the congregation, Joseph Ratzinger, the church's watchdog committee of morals and orthodoxy had discovered new purpose and new energy. Rome was flexing its muscles. In the decade of Pell's membership, the congregation would ban books, silence theologians, excommunicate Marxists and find fresh ways of excoriating homosexuality: "objectively disordered external conduct" which nations have an obligation to discriminate against "in order to protect the common good." In the course of these deliberations, Pell and Ratzinger became friends, a key friendship the Australian was suitably modest about. In time, he would help gather the votes that made Ratzinger pope. Rome also made Pell a consultor to the Pontifical Council for the Family and a member of the Pontifical Council for Justice and Peace. The former led the Vatican campaign against contraception. The latter battled left-wing political tendencies in the church. Pell began spending more time in Rome.

John Paul showed no purpose over paedophiles. In 1989 he denied bishops the right to sack abusers. Bishops could suspend but not laicise. That remained – and remains – the prerogative of Rome. Paedophile priests operated for most of John Paul's reign knowing it was essentially impossible to be thrown out of the church against their will. The historic apologies John Paul issued for the past sins of the church in these years did not include an apology to abused children. He was deaf and blind to complaints that Father Marcial Maciel Degollado, an ultra-conservative with a miraculous talent for raising cash, was addicted to morphine and abusing children. John Paul's cardinal secretary of state, Angelo Sodano, blocked investigations into Maciel's crimes. He also blocked an investigation – initiated by Ratzinger – into the long paedophilic career of the archbishop of Vienna, Hans Groër. Groër was forced to resign in 1995 but allowed to live out his years as a cardinal. He died accused of abusing more than 2000 young men. In a letter to the bishops of the United States in 1993, John Paul deplored the press exposing errant priests to "the ridicule of public opinion" and for forgetting that even the worst might be raised up again through prayer. "One cannot acquiesce," wrote His Holiness, "in treating moral evil as an occasion for sensationalism."

John Paul had his faults. One was a weakness for flattery. Pell's flattery of the man was brazen. He wrote of John Paul leading the forces of the one true God into battle against the forces of darkness. In the story of the fall of the Berlin Wall, he cast John Paul as a heroic figure of the stature of Churchill, de Gaulle and a couple of the greatest popes of history:

> Certainly his role, with Ronald Reagan, in the collapse of Communism dwarfs the efforts of Pope Leo the Great and then Pope Gregory the Great in the fifth and sixth centuries to defend Rome and the remnants of the Roman Empire in the West from the depreda-

> tions of the barbarians ... it is not surprising that one magazine I
> saw spoke of the Pope as a second Moses!

How could he not admire a pope who demonstrated in the twentieth century the historic role of Catholicism as the bulwark of civilisation? As a fourteen-year-old boy in Ballarat he had signed on for just this mission. In the pages of *AD 2000*, Pell was keeping the faith by confronting feminists, neo-pagans, masturbation, drugs, pornography, "mail-order divorce," television, Marxists, modernism, "theological confusion and divisions among our intelligentsia," prosperity ("too much sugar"), proportionalism, "the spread of gay propaganda," pre-marital sex, contraception, abortion, sex education in schools, *Brides of Christ* (the ABC's "popular religious soapie"), poor liturgy, "the soft nihilism which has settled over Western Europe and the English-speaking world," the culture of death, Peter Singer ("King Herod's propaganda chief in Australia, our most notorious messenger of death") and again and again and again the false doctrine of the primacy of conscience: "However inauspicious the omens, however hostile the clime, the task of each one of us is to preserve the Catholic tradition, the centrality of God, of Christ's love as God is lived and loved in the Church that is led by the Pope, the Bishop of Rome."

*

Pell was in his sixth year as a bishop when the police came for Father Ridsdale. By this time arrests were happening often. The first paedophile priest to be sent to jail in Melbourne in living memory was Michael Glennon in 1978. Shame and respect were not working as they once did to silence victims. A new breed of police was no longer willing to put faith before duty. The religious beginning to appear in handcuffs came from all faiths but most, by far, were Catholic. Professor Patrick Parkinson of Sydney University, a lawyer and expert on child protection, told the Victorian inquiry:

If you compare the statistics, I would say conservatively that there is six times as much abuse in the Catholic Church as all the other churches in Australia combined …

Putting things into perspective, the Catholic Church is the largest Church, and it also had a great deal of involvement in school work and orphanages, children's homes and so on. Even still, the levels of abuse in the Catholic Church are strikingly out of proportion with any other church …

Victoria Police began Operation Paradox in the early 1990s: a hotline open for a few weeks each year for victims to report their sexual abuse as children. In August 1992 a call came to Operation Paradox from a man who said Father Gerald Ridsdale had raped him at the altar at St Malachy's in Edenhope in the 1970s. Half-a-dozen more victims were soon tracked down. Police found the priest working as a chaplain at a Catholic psychiatric hospital in Sydney and brought him back to Melbourne. He put up no resistance. According to the *Age*, "The tone of Father Ridsdale's police interview suggests he was enormously relieved when the silence shrouding his misdemeanours was shattered. So relieved, he confessed to other sex crimes of which he had been neither suspected nor accused."

Parishioners loved Father Gerry. He was big, charming, "churchy" but boisterous. Busy mothers of big families were happy to hand their sons to him for camping trips and fishing expeditions. A favourite destination for Ridsdale was an opal miner's block he had at White Cliffs in New South Wales. He began abusing kids the moment he was ordained. An anonymous church source speaking to *OutRage* magazine claimed Bishop O'Collins had "commissioned a psychiatric report on Father Ridsdale in 1966, barely five years after his ordination." He abused children in Mildura and Swan Hill on the Murray, and Warrnambool on the Great Ocean Road. One of the altar boys in Warrnambool complained, so Ridsdale was moved to the parish and school of St Alipius in Ballarat, where he was immediately assaulting children. According to a report of the Victorian

Child Exploitation Squad, one of the altar boys complained in 1971 to the new bishop: "Mulkearns replied: 'It will be all right, son.' [The boy] states he was then moved from Ridsdale's roster and placed on to Mulkearns' roster and on to the roster of two other priests."

After his year in the presbytery with Pell, Ridsdale left to continue the itinerant criminal life that was the pattern of his career: abuse, exposure, "treatment," relocation to a fresh parish and more abuse. Priests gossip. When one disappears suddenly from his post, the priests of the diocese soon know what's up. It takes only a few phone calls. The bishop knows, the priests know and the only people out of the loop are the Catholic faithful in the next parish. They could be remarkably forgiving when the new priest in town turned out to be an abuser. After Ridsdale left Inglewood suddenly one night, the people of that sleepy gold-rush town didn't want to press charges. "He was seen as a congenial and effective priest," the *Age* reported. "They did not want him pilloried: they just wanted him out of town." Through all these shifts, Mulkearns never reported Ridsdale to the police, and when the police in turn heard complaints they left the priest to be dealt with by the church.

Ridsdale was balding and tubby by this time. He had grown a bushy beard. "Come here and give us a hug," he would say. "Fozzie Bear loves you." His good cheer and predatory energy were undimmed. The *Age* reported how the priest insinuated himself into "Stephen's" family:

> He would appear mid-morning and take up a position in a corner of the lounge room, a St Kilda football beanie on his head, and drink beer with Stephen's father and watch *World of Sport*, a ragged, meandering television sports show. The Sunday roast was served when the show finished, and Stephen's mother would ask the priest to say grace. Afterwards Ridsdale would take Stephen fishing, masturbate him and perform oral sex upon him. "We can't work out how he came to be part of our family, but he did."

After a sudden departure from Edenhope in 1979, he was sent to Mort-lake, from where, within days, complaints were being made to Mulkearns. So he was given a desk job at the Catholic Information Centre in Sydney, where he found more victims. Then it was back briefly to Ballarat before a visit to Jemez Springs, New Mexico, where, since 1947, the Servants of the Paraclete had been trying to wean broken priests off alcohol, drugs, women, men and children. Almost from the start, the founder of this out-fit had been warning the church that paedophiles couldn't be cured and should never be returned to parishes. He was usually ignored but not in Ridsdale's case. On his return to Australia in 1991, the paedophile priest was made chaplain at a Catholic psychiatric hospital in an old stone house on the Hawkesbury River west of Sydney.

Ridsdale had a cover story for his family. His nephew David recalls: "He said he was very good with finances and was being moved from parish to parish to clean up the books." The priest in the family, the shining light of the big Ridsdale clan, began abusing David when he was eleven and the crimes against the child continued for five years. No one knew. The boy threw himself into the YMCA, where he did well as a youth leader. "But nobody knew how screwed up my real life was." David was married with a child when he decided something had to be done about his uncle. He knew nothing of Ridsdale's life of crime, only that he had been assaulted and raped. He didn't want him exposed. "I was afraid it might kill my grandmother." He wanted something done qui-etly. He had made an anonymous call to the police sometime earlier. Nothing happened. So he turned to Bishop Pell. He had grown up in Bal-larat calling this man George. He thought of him as a family friend and a powerful man in the church who could do something tactful and effec-tive about his uncle.

He rang Mentone in early February 1993 to tell Pell about the abuse at his uncle's hands. "His reaction was so totally unexpected," he would tell 60 Minutes a decade later. "He didn't respond to anything I said. He sort of cut me off." Pell seemed angry and somehow blaming him for being the cause of that distress. He remembers Pell saying: "David, you have a young family, you will have to make purchases like houses and cars." David was confused. "All of a sudden I just stopped and went, 'George, I'm totally lost. Can you please tell me what you were trying to say here?'" He has never since wavered in his claim that Pell replied: "I want to know what it will take to keep you quiet." David was furious. "It changed everything," he told *60 Minutes*. "I said, 'Fuck you and fuck everything you stand for,' and I hung up." Then he rang the police. He also spoke that day to his sisters. One, Bernie, remembered him saying Pell wanted to know what it would take "to make it go away." Trish remembered her brother saying: "The bastard tried to offer me a bribe."

Pell contests David Ridsdale's account of the conversation. He does not deny offering assistance of some kind, a gesture he believes was misunderstood. "An offer of help is not the same as a bribe." In a statutory declaration he swore after *60 Minutes* went to air in 2002, Pell said:

> When I received the phone call, I was aware that allegations of criminal conduct were being made against Ridsdale, that they involved offences against a number of children and that the allegations included offences against members of Ridsdale's family. I had no reason to believe that Ridsdale was innocent of the allegations ... it was alleged that I said to David words to the effect, "What will it take to keep it quiet?" I emphatically and totally deny having said these words or any words to that effect. I emphatically and totally deny the allegation that I made any attempt to buy David's silence.

David Ridsdale had another surprise when he rang the police that afternoon. "Did you know what we were planning to do today?" they asked. His uncle was in Melbourne and about to be charged. Now they held off and next day David Ridsdale spent some hours with them giving his statement. At a special sitting of the Melbourne Magistrates' Court that night, Gerald Francis Ridsdale, fifty-nine, was charged with twenty-seven counts of indecently assaulting boys in the late 1970s and early 1980s in Edenhope, Apollo

Bay, Inglewood and Ballarat. The police believed this list would only be the start. They made sure the press and television cameras were waiting when the old priest turned up to court four months later. What they couldn't have imagined was that he would arrive in the company of Bishop Pell.

Pell's presence that day went unremarked by the press. He would be archbishop of Melbourne before he was asked to explain his presence at Ridsdale's side. It was no more, he said, than "a gesture of support" for a "brother priest who made terrible mistakes." He would be archbishop of Sydney before he was accused of attempting to silence Ridsdale's nephew. In May 1993 the only people enraged by Pell's role in Ridsdale's first trial were victims of abuse by priests. Pell had declined Ridsdale's lawyer's request to go into the witness box but he must have known his presence would count in the eyes of the magistrate. Mr Julian Fitz-Gerald could see the paedophile in the white suit had the support of a bishop. After pleading guilty to assaulting nine boys in his care, Ridsdale was sentenced to only three months' imprisonment. That light sentence further infuriated victims. They rang the police. Ridsdale soon faced a further 151 offences against fourteen boys. He had become the face of paedophilia in the Catholic Church.

Victims also rang lawyers. The first wave of lawsuits against the church began after Ridsdale. Lawyers told the *Age* that the "cold comfort" of his light sentence spurred victims "to hold the church morally and financially accountable through civil legal action." And victims rang Broken Rites, which, for the past year, had been building a data bank of paedophile religious of all faiths that would become an indispensable resource for campaigners, the press and lawyers. After Ridsdale, money and calls poured in. When Broken Rites went online a few years later, they honoured this turning point in the group's fortunes by putting on their homepage a shot of Pell, sombre in black clericals, walking Ridsdale in his cheap white suit and dark glasses into court. It's still there.

*

Battle-hardened Gerry Cudmore, chaplain in the Vietnam War, began his time as vicar-general of the archdiocese of Melbourne doing all the church demanded: he shifted paedophile priests to fresh parishes; lied to cover the moves; heard complaints and took no action; worked to discredit witnesses; and blocked investigations. This was how Archbishop Little dealt with these crimes. But Cudmore was deeply troubled. He told one victim: "When a priest offended, they were sent away for six months. They would come back and say, 'I've prayed to God for strength and I feel that I have got the strength now and it's okay.' And we took them at their word. Then they went out and reoffended." After Ridsdale, writs started arriving. Cudmore asked Helen Last to lunch in 1994. They had met through her work at the Royal Women's Hospital with survivors – first women and later men – of abuse within Christian communities. Last told me:

> He sat there all through lunch holding his head in his hands. He said: "There are thirty-two writs on the archbishop and people keep rolling up to the front reception desk and serving them. It's just too much, too much for us. I don't know what to do. I've got so many victims beating my door down. They're constantly turning up asking to see me. I don't know how to help them. And the offenders are still in the parishes where these people are coming from, the priest is still there and I don't know what to do, where to go with that. I need help with this. When can you start?"

The Pastoral Response Office of the archdiocese opened in East Melbourne in July 1995, with Helen Last as coordinator. It couldn't remove priests or offer compensation, but it could help victims and their parishes in the aftermath of a paedophile priest. This was a radical program of advocacy, pastoral care, counselling and referrals to lawyers and police. The office was active in ways the church had never been: it went out and looked for victims. In November 1995 more than 200 people attended Pastoral Response programs in Rosanna, where the paedophile Des Gannon had been priest for thirteen years before being pulled out by Cudmore – for "health reasons" – and then jailed. At least four more trials have followed. Last was appalled by what she learnt in these months in Melbourne. "This work was like crawling through the sewers without a gas mask. It was just shit, just horrific abuse."

Cudmore publicly declared paedophile priests criminals and in early 1996 delivered what appears to be the first public apology to their victims made by a senior Catholic in Australia:

> We must live with the pain and shame of what has happened. We deeply regret the fact that priests have been involved in sexual abuse, and on behalf of the whole church we offer the victims of such abuse a sincere apology … The exceptional trust given to Catholic clergy confers exceptional power. We are bewildered that this power has become so destructive in the lives of some, and we are determined to ensure that the same does not happen to others.

A few weeks later he was in court to see Father Anthony Bongiorno committed to stand trial for assaulting three young boys. Broken Rites reported: "As people left the courtroom, the vicar-general of the Melbourne archdiocese (Monsignor Gerald Cudmore) was at the rear of the courtroom, handing out a statement inviting victims of church sexual abuse to contact the archdiocese." Last remembers him going to other trials. "It was the first time ever a vicar-general went to the Melbourne Magistrates' Court to stand with the victims and let them cry on his shoulder."

Archbishop Little was buckling under the strain as he tried, very late in the day, to address this scandal. Helen Last recalled: "He was becoming more and more unwell. His nervous system was breaking down. His physical ability and emotional ability – I won't even talk about spiritual ability – to withstand this constant pressure was breaking down." Cudmore told her there were forces trying to push her out of the Pastoral Response Office. He reassured Last: "I have told Little if you go, I go." Then, without warning, on 16 July 1996 Frank Little was gone and George Pell was named archbishop.

Rome made no effort to disguise the coup. Usually weeks are spent appearing, at least, to canvass Australian bishops before naming the new man. But within hours of Little "resigning" on health grounds, the Vatican ambassador to Australia announced John Paul had chosen Pell to take his place. Little told Last: "I have had to drink from the poisoned cup." Across Melbourne, Catholics expressed shock, surprise and, in some quarters, great satisfaction. Little allowed himself a wry joke when asked by the press what exactly was wrong with his health: "Will I start with the ingrown toenails?" Pell nailed his colours to the mast. He promised to be just and reasonable. He acknowledged there were Catholics disappointed by this turn of events: "It is quite impossible to please everybody all the time. I will be working hard to try and maintain traditional loyalty to the Papacy and to the Catholic tradition. I believe in the Papacy."

The lumbering figure walking the length of Melbourne's Royal Exhibition Building to the sound of Handel's "Hallelujah Chorus" on the night of 16 August 1996 was in better health than he had been for years. He had shed weight. A little grey was showing under the mitre but, all things being equal, Pell had twenty years ahead of him to fulfil Rome's mandate. He had been a contentious figure inside the church for years but his appointment to Melbourne exposed him to wider public scrutiny. Australia was beginning to pay attention. That he broke the mould made him interesting. Catholic archbishops hadn't sounded like him for forty years. He was deliberate rather than graceful. He had the bearing of a football coach rather than a divine. His face was chunky and his mouth surprisingly small. His voice was masculine but oddly refined: Oxford laid over Ballarat. That he had so little charm was arresting. He seemed not to try to win people over. He was not a persuader. He spoke at that slow, clear pace headmasters and doctors use, a pace that says: if you fail to obey, you don't have the excuse of misunderstanding me. The threat is in the rhythm. He had a powerful man's habit of often seeming to focus his attention elsewhere. He didn't hug. He flinched from the attentions of the devout. He appeared to have sex well bricked up inside himself with the determination of a professional celibate.

A week after Rome announced his appointment, a court in Melbourne lifted orders suppressing media reports of the paedophile ring of St Alipius. The press was ready and waiting. The stories were sober, shocking and detailed. Victims put their names to stories of abuse and betrayal. The archbishop-designate found himself in the thick of an ugly controversy. It was reported for the first time that he had lived in the St Alipius presbytery and walked Father Ridsdale to court. Stephen Woods, abused by Brother Dowlan for years when he was a little boy and raped when he turned to Ridsdale for help, called for a royal commission and for Pell's resignation: "He should have known, he ought to have known what was going on." Pell held fast. "I was a junior curate," he said. "I was wetter behind the ears then than I am now. You didn't suspect people of those things then." The premier of Victoria, Jeff Kennett, rejected calls for a royal commission. He told the *Australian*: "It's a matter for the Catholic Church to resolve itself with its constituency and with the community." He had a tougher message for the new man in private: "If you don't fix it, I will."

As Pell began to speak – apparently for the first time – about the abuse of children by priests, he said the "hurts and wounds" of the victims were his highest priority. But he was fearless in his defence of priests: male, celibate and sacred. He rejected talk of a paedophile culture in the church. There were errant priests. Some were worse than others: "The very worst cases, almost sordid beyond belief, are not the whole picture among the offenders." He promised not to hide their crimes by moving them around. "It is universally recognised that it is an inappropriate way to deal with the problem." But he made no undertaking to hunt them out, to go into the schools and parishes of Melbourne to find how bad the situation may be. In one odd interview with the *Herald Sun* he seemed to say he would rather not know: "If a priest comes to me, I don't want him to tell me if he is guilty or not guilty, unless he insists on telling me. In which case I would have to act on the information." He declared celibacy not to blame: "The great majority of paedophiles are married people. All the literature suggests that celibacy is not directly related to paedophilia." He began to birch the media – as he would for the next twenty years – for "disproportionate and repetitious" reporting of the sex crimes of the clergy. He promised victims he would not play "legal games" but wanted it understood that the church was not a soft touch. "If we believe we are being sued for things that are not our responsibility or where we dispute or deny the allegations, we will certainly fight it." Pell conceded the church's approach to the abuse crisis had been a bit "spotty." "We are going to have to do better in the future."

Television forced the church forward. In June 1993 *Compass* revealed that the church had taken out insurance against paedophile priests and prepared the secret, hard-line protocol of 1992. Within days the bishops' committee began working on a protocol more sympathetic to victims and tougher on priests. But it came to a halt because a provision in the draft threatened to expel from the church all priests breaking their vow of celibacy: "Priests, religious and church workers need to be aware that sexual abuse or misconduct on their part is not compatible with ongoing ministry in the church." The committee of bishops – renamed Professional Standards – resumed work in 1994 under Geoffrey Robinson, one of Sydney's auxiliary bishops and a late but passionate convert to the cause of justice for victims. Progress was slow. Robinson told colleagues: "People think turning around the church on an issue like this is like turning around a big ship. It's not, it's an armada."

Lawyers who took up the fight for victims found no way through the formidable defences the church has built around its wealth. Pell's promise not to play "legal games" was entirely empty: the Catholic Church and its lawyers play such games ruthlessly. They will not admit priests are employees. They refuse to take responsibility for priests' abuse. And they lock up the wealth of the church in trusts that litigants can't access. As the bishops began to search for ways of offering justice to victims, they might simply have decided to stop the games and let the victims sue. That was never contemplated. Keeping the whole thing out of court and in the hands of the church was fundamental to the protocol called Towards Healing, which was to be unveiled at the bishops' conference in late 1996. The church would assess the needs of victims; offer help and counselling; and perhaps give an ex gratia payment by way of compensation. The victims would really have no choice: either accept what was offered, or fight an almost impossible battle through the courts against a determined and very wealthy opponent, their church.

Pell was taking his own soundings at the big end of town. At lunch one day the governor of Victoria, Richard McGarvie, gave him some advice. "You are going to have to deal with this problem resolutely. If you don't, it will bleed you dry for years – emotionally, and more importantly than that, it will bleed away the good standing of the church." Pell told the Victorian inquiry: "He made the suggestion that what we needed was something like a Catholic royal commission, to get a senior person to judge and evaluate these crimes, give him independence, and that would be the best way forward." Pell canvassed the idea with Kennett and the police. Both were happy to leave it to the church. Pell's scheme would cover only priests in the parishes of Melbourne. He hired a senior barrister, Peter O'Callaghan QC, to be his "independent commissioner" and on 30 October 1996 called a press conference to announce what he had named the Melbourne Response. And on that occasion he took what he regarded as a step of great significance for an archbishop. He apologised:

> On behalf of the Catholic Church of the archdiocese of Melbourne I would like to make a sincere, unreserved and public apology, first of all to the victims of sexual abuse but also to the people of the archdiocese for the actions of those Catholic clergy and others who have betrayed the trust placed in them by their parishioners.

Lawyers battling to sue the church were scathing about Pell's Melbourne Response. One man representing forty-five clients called it "a crude package of measures designed to entice victims to accept a dramatic reduction in their proper entitlements." He dismissed the $50,000 cap Pell placed on payouts as "an insult to victims." The *Age* also condemned the cap for not giving victims what they might need to deal with "problems in later life such as alcohol or drug addiction, and consequent loss of income and family breakdown." The newspaper declared: "The time for tokens is over." Pell did not budge.

The Melbourne Response had one distinct advantage over the bishops' national scheme: a more direct pathway to compensation. But there were hazards everywhere for victims knocking on its door. First they had to promise not to disclose any information "in relation to the Panel's deliberations." That was understood by many to be a demand for absolute secrecy. Whether they were encouraged to go to the police would be a point of great controversy. They were certainly told that if they did, the Melbourne Response would have to cease work on their cases. Victims were not given lawyers. Priests were. Despite talk of O'Callaghan being a Catholic royal commissioner, he had none of the powers a commissioner has to ferret out documents and compel witnesses to answer questions. Stripped of the rhetoric, he was a lawyer working for the archbishop of Melbourne. His decisions were final. He was not obliged to give his reasons. Victims who convinced him of their bona fides were passed to two separate panels. One arranged counselling. The other offered money. The cap imposed by Pell meant even child victims of repeated rape would receive no more than $50,000. Payments came with no admissions of liability. Nothing was paid until victims signed away all claims they might have at any time in the future against the church. If they hesitated to accept what was offered, they were told this was "a realistic alternative to litigation that will otherwise be strenuously defended." Pell and O'Callaghan both thought the work of the Melbourne Response would be done fairly quickly. "That was reflected in the fact that the terms and conditions of my original brief were for a period of six months," O'Callaghan told the Victorian inquiry. He is still there.

The bishops were furious with Pell. They would never forgive him for breaking ranks. "He was going his way and bugger the rest of Australia," said Bishop Pat Power. "But he's not a team player in that sense at all, unless he's the captain of the team and everyone else is following him." The bishops did not like him. All but a few of them deplored his brand of Catholicism. And no matter how high he rose in the years ahead, they would never elect him leader of the bishops' conference. Why he struck out on his own with the Melbourne Response has been the subject of intense speculation ever since. There are those in the church who say this was the bully they knew at Werribee. Pell blames the bishops themselves for dithering. "In light of the urgent need for an effective system to respond to victims of abuse and the uncertainty at that stage about initiatives for a national response, I moved quickly." He was one of the first in the world to put such a system in place, an honour he has often claimed. And the Melbourne Response offered him what Towards Healing could never give: control.

*

Pell was making changes. Cudmore decided to bow out. He didn't think he could work with Pell. The new vicar-general was one of Pell's close friends, Father Denis Hart, the man who had organised the magnificent ceremony of consecration in the Exhibition Building. In November the rector and all the teaching staff of Corpus Christi quit in protest when Pell ordered radical changes at the seminary. Priests were to be taught "to pray better, to celebrate the sacraments more devoutly and pray the word of God more devoutly, especially by example." A little further down the track he appointed another friend and conservative, Monsignor Peter Elliott, back in Melbourne after ten years in Rome, as vicar for religious education. There was dread in the classrooms. Dogma was back. Nothing else Pell did in these years caused such apprehension in Melbourne. With Santamaria's daughter Mary Helen Woods he wrote a book to be used in all schools in the archdiocese: *Issues of Faith and Morals*. Its preface read: "This book is written with the conviction that nothing is to be gained by hiding the severity of Christ's teaching."

At that time the church was telling the Wood royal commission in New South Wales about the great work of Helen Last's Pastoral Response Office. Last gave evidence to Wood. The message was that whatever mistakes had been made in the past, the church was pioneering ways of caring for the victims of clerical sex abuse. Alas, by the time Jim Wood commended her office in his final report, Pell had shut it down. One reason was the unhappy "aftermath" forum organised in Oakleigh, the parish of insatiable paedophile Kevin O'Donnell, who was living in retirement after serving a prison sentence, though still a priest with the title pastor emeritus.

The church had known for nearly forty years that Father O'Donnell was a danger to children. A young scout complained about him in 1958 and was told by Bishop Arthur Fox: "You should never speak about this to anyone. It would be a mortal sin to discuss it." That was in the parish of Dandenong, where O'Donnell abused children for another ten years. He spent the next seven doing the same in Hastings. There was more to O'Donnell than abuse and intimidation: he had a shrewd eye for real estate and made the church a good deal of money. At the age of sixty he reached Oakleigh, an old city engulfed by the Melbourne suburbs, and began abusing the children in his presbytery, in the church, the church hall, at Sacred Heart Primary, in cars, at the drive-in and in a weatherboard shack he had at the beach. O'Donnell demanded lots of sex: police would call him a two-a-day man. The headmaster of Sacred Heart tried for years to persuade the archdiocese to remove this domineering priest simply for being so rude to the children. He failed. O'Donnell was in Oakleigh when Pell became auxiliary bishop in 1986. Oakleigh was in his bailiwick. According to an *Age* investigation by Peter Ellingsen, 1986 was also the year the archdiocese was warned once again about this priest: "A nun who had counselled one of his Dandenong victims wrote that year a letter telling the archdiocese of what she had learnt. Still, O'Donnell was left at Oakleigh for a further six years." The archdiocese told Ellingsen it had no records of complaints about O'Donnell before his retirement in 1992. The police came for him soon after. He was charged with indecently assaulting twelve boys – only a representative sample of his crimes – and served fifteen months in prison, a light sentence because of his great age. He had been released only a few weeks before the parishioners of Oakleigh gathered to discuss this appalling saga with their archbishop in February 1997.

Waiting in the presbytery to see Pell before the forum began were Chrissie and Anthony Foster. O'Donnell had raped two of their daughters when the girls were about five years old. At this point the Fosters knew only about his attacks on their eldest child, Emma. They had yet to discover he had raped Katie too. Emma was now fifteen. Her life had collapsed. She was anorexic, depressed, suicidal, and in and out of a psychiatric unit for adolescents. The Fosters had brought two pictures of the child to show Pell: one with her receiving her confirmation certificate from Pell and another of her sitting in the backyard after her most recent suicide attempt in a nearby laneway. The Fosters sat waiting on a hard bench in a cluttered room. They heard Pell outside the door asking the new parish priest about them: "Are they friends?" The archbishop took a red leather armchair and there ensued a conversation Chrissie Foster described in her book, *Hell on the Way to Heaven*, as "both gruelling and unpleasant."

> When Anthony mentioned the Church had known about O'Donnell's paedophilia for many decades, Archbishop Pell said: "That was before my time" …
>
> We believed Archbishop Pell knew O'Donnell assaulted Emma. But Anthony repeated the facts for him, just in case.
>
> "I hope you can substantiate that in court," came the words that shook us most. Anthony winced …
>
> The discussion moved quickly to the new scheme for complaints and compensation. Anthony said it was a cost-saving measure, unfair and to the victims' detriment. "It might look good on paper but as people involved in this, as victims, it all looks very shallow. Part of the reason is we see this cap and we see these restrictions –"
>
> Archbishop Pell interjected: "If you don't like what we're doing, take us to court."

The meeting did not recover. A little before it ended, the Fosters showed Pell the photographs of their daughter. "That's nice," he said of the confirmation shot. Then they showed him the other:

> Anthony gave him the image of Emma with bloodied wrists and arms. I held my breath, hopeful that we could reach this man on a deeper level … Archbishop Pell, however, peered at it for a moment and with an unchanged expression said casually: "Mmm … she's

changed, hasn't she?" He handed the picture back to us. We couldn't believe his response. He was the first person we'd shown the image to. It was too distressing for anyone we knew to see. It did not disturb the archbishop. Not a grimace or a frown.

Pell would make many baffled apologies for their half-hour together in the presbytery. He told the Victorian inquiry: "No matter what I said or did, it seemed to make things worse. I am sorry for whatever I did to upset them at this meeting. It was certainly not my intention to upset them. I wanted to help them." But he has never apologised to the Fosters.

They made their separate ways to the school hall over the road. On a hot night in suburban Melbourne a roomful of Catholics was pleased their new archbishop had come to hear them. They were victims, parents of victims and concerned parishioners. Pell had asked Last to give him some speaking points. "He didn't know what to say to them." The press was banned. So was taping the proceedings. But notes taken by several attending the forum, including the Fosters, were later compiled into an eighteen-page record of the disaster that unfolded as people began to tell Pell about their terrible experiences:

> My son was interfered with when making his first confession at Sacred Heart Parish ... I would be late picking up my son from school – I'd say, "Go into the presbytery, you'll be safe." I will not rest easy until I can once again say, "Go into the presbytery, you'll be safe." George, it's in your hands ...
>
> Four years ago [we] found out both of our two sons [were] abused by a member of Parish ... at the time one was about eight years old, the other a bit older. Now they are thirty and thirty-two. Over that period of time they have suffered and we are suffering. Can you imagine our suffering – what on earth must it be like for those children?
>
> We are all Catholics and since birth have been indoctrinated to believe and trust in the priests and religious. So the denial that we are talking about and the idea that our priests could be doing some-

thing like this is almost outside the parameters of our thinking ...
And that is why it is hard for this to come out in any way. That is
why what is happening instead, in this parish and in lots of others,
from people I have talked to, people have just decided, "Bugger it,
this is too hard" – they are just walking away. They are walking
away, they don't want anything to do with it and they don't know
how to fight it.

Pell kept his head down, taking notes. The people in the room became
confused and hurt. Everything stopped. Pell was asked: "Why are you
writing? Have you heard everything? Do you know how much pain is in
this group?" He said: "I am writing because I want to reply to specific
points." But now he began to speak. He was trying hard but seemed lost
in the desert of his own feelings. He pleaded for understanding.

> PELL: I grew up in a family. I am close to nephews and nieces etc. I
> have always tried to help. I would be the first to admit that my
> response to problems would be qualitatively different from that
> of a parent to his or her own child. I recognise that, but I try to
> be sympathetic.

But then the father of a child who had been raped, flailing about as he
tried to express his disappointment at the way Pell had set up the Melbourne Response without consulting victims, earned from the archbishop
a stern rebuke.

> PELL: I don't find your tone a bit helpful.
> PARISHIONER: The man is hurting.
> PELL: Yes, and so am I. I don't need to be hectored by yourself
> before I can feel sympathy. I feel the greatest sympathy for your
> children and I feel the greatest sympathy for yourself ...
> PARISHIONER: My brother is one of the gentlest people. He is angry
> ... I expect a man of your position to understand anger, depres-
> sion, feel isolation, hurt and God knows that people are extremely

tolerant. He is a mixture of all these emotions and you don't find
it helpful?

The meeting had an underlying purpose made clear to Pell again and
again: "Get rid of these people, these criminals – do something about it!
That is why we are here this evening." And they wanted Pell to understand that the church had to take the initiative because it was so hard for
children to speak and took so long for victims to find their voice. The
church had to investigate, to find the priests and take action. They were
getting close to the heart of the problem:

> PARISHIONER: What we're asking you to do is go and find the
> paedophiles and get them out of the church. You actually have
> to go and look for them, because the kids cannot talk. They've
> been traumatised and tortured so much that they cannot talk
> about this. You have to go and look for them. Until you come to
> that point we are miles apart. You have to go and look for the
> paedophiles and you have to get them out of the parishes some-
> how. If that means changing the structure of the church to
> accommodate it, then that is the only way to protect the chil-
> dren. You cannot sit back and wait for the allegations.
>
> PELL: I'm sorry but I think that's bit of a cop-out, putting all the
> onus on me. You have an obligation to report what you know
> and encourage other parents to report what they know and to go
> to the appropriate authorities – and if you come to me, I will put
> the proper processes in place to deal with those. I've got a crucial
> part in this, [but] so have other people.

The meeting began naming priests. Chrissie Foster wrote that the mention of Searson's name, and the names of the abusive priests of Doveton,
had the archbishop thundering: "It's all gossip until it's proven in court
and I don't listen to gossip." The accusation stung his audience. They had
information that was not being acted on. When would the church do

something? What standard of proof did Pell require? When he argued for proof on at least the balance of probabilities, he was met with angry disbelief:

> PARISHIONER: To us that is still outrageously high. It's kids we're trying to protect here ... if there is any risk to a child in the parish from a priest or anyone else in authority ... if there is a display of behaviour which would tend to indicate that there is a possibility of something happening to a child, then you shift the priest from parish duties. It's so patently obvious to a parent ... the standard of proof has to be care for the kids.

That was not Pell's view: even sending a priest on leave was "a significant step" that could not be taken without "some level of real evidence." He angrily rejected the suggestion that he was part of a cover-up.

> PELL: I am not duck-shoving, I'm not interested in saving anybody's skin, I'm interested only in dealing justly with people. If there is evidence that an independent investigator reckons is realistic, I will remove him as a precaution ... what you've got to realise is that sometimes people can honestly make a mountain out of a molehill, and also some evil people will maliciously concoct stories from go to whoa, and that has already happened. We have to be just to people who are accused, and we will be – but if there is evidence, they will be removed.

Pell sided once with his audience against Rome. Asked why O'Donnell, a convicted paedophile, was still a priest, he replied: "It would help our situation immensely if some of these people could be laicised against their will." But history made it impossible. "In the past there have been tyrannical bishops who would laicise priests at the drop of a hat. Rome, in its wisdom, is dealing with past problems." He spoke about O'Donnell. He told them he had visited him in his prison hospital and heard him mutter,

"I'm sorry … I'm sorry … I'm sorry." Why, Chrissie Foster wondered, was he telling them about this mawkish scene? What was O'Donnell sorry for? Pell's final recommendation was prayer:

> I'm convinced that a very significant percentage of our problems in the church, right across the board, come from when people give up praying, and praying regularly. And that goes for all of us. If we want healing, undoubtedly that involves some amount of regular prayer.

Chrissie Foster wrote: "So the meeting wrapped up, with us feeling some kind of instinctive guilt. We felt flat, empty, defeated – as if we had achieved nothing." This was Pell's third parish forum and he never held another. He told the Victorian inquiry: "I was not keen to continue them precisely because of the bad experience at the third meeting … where people were condemning priests here there and everywhere … people were cross – it did not contribute to making things better."

*

Pell had a stack of files about difficult priests. Frank Little may have put nothing in writing but Cudmore did. "He was a great note-taker," Helen Last told me. "He kept very good files." Last says they were held in a special filing cabinet by his desk and contained correspondence about accusations of abuse; records of dealings with parishioners, victims and police; plus Cudmore's own memoranda on the cases. Ellingsen reported in the *Age*: "By the time Cudmore stepped down in 1996, the filing cabinet had gone from holding one file to 120, and sex abuse was the biggest and most difficult problem that the vicar-general faced." Cudmore left this material behind when he handed over to his successor, Denis Hart, who is now archbishop of Melbourne. Hart does not dispute their existence. "Monsignor Cudmore's files and records were available to Monsignor Hart on becoming vicar-general," his spokesman told me. "The files related to nineteen priests against whom complaints were made between 1978 and

1996." What was available to Hart was available to Pell. At some point the archbishop handed the files to O'Callaghan. He took no action himself against two priests whose failings had been extensively documented by Cudmore. Pell would tell the Victorian inquiry that he still knew of no reason to pull Searson out of Doveton and remained unaware of the file kept on Billy Baker of North Richmond.

As a young man, the former priest Phil O'Donnell had the unhappy experience of being curate to both Searson and Baker. He told the Victorian inquiry:

> There had been multiple, consistent allegations about Father Baker from the early 1960s. In fact I personally read the letters from his file that probably I should not have had access to, but they were given to me by the then vicar-general, Monsignor Gerry Cudmore, who was particularly frustrated with having to deal with this absolute crisis.

Phil O'Donnell caught Baker grooming a boy in the late 1970s and alerted the child's parents. Frank Little rebuffed both the child's parents and then two lawyers from the parish, threatening defamation and calling their complaints about Baker "despicable." Baker continued to attack children, first in Eltham and then in North Richmond, where parents eventually refused to allow their sons to be his altar boys. Complaints reached Cudmore in 1993 but according to the Sunday Herald Sun the then auxiliary bishop Peter Connors dismissed them as "only rumour and hearsay." A few weeks before Pell became archbishop in 1996, Phil O'Donnell wrote to Cudmore to say that Baker was now under police investigation yet still in his parish:

> This leads me to yet another dimension of this tragic scandal. I find it difficult to reconcile how the church authorities have, or at least should have, specific allegations against priests, and that these priests are still on active archdiocesan appointment. I do have to

question whether the competent ecclesial authorities have the will to address the sad reality of clergy child sexual abuse.

Pell told the Victorian inquiry he did not see the letter and was unaware of the police investigation: "If I had known he was being investigated by the police, he would have been stood down immediately." He took no action. O'Callaghan stood Baker down in June 1997. The priest was jailed for four years in 1999 after pleading guilty to sixteen counts of indecent assault and one of gross indecency. Pell issued an apology to Baker's victims. Baker was not defrocked until 2012.

At least Father Ronald Pickering was no longer a danger to the children of Melbourne. He vanished from the parish of St James, Gardenvale, one night in 1993 and fled to England. Pickering was another of the problem priests Pell inherited when he became auxiliary bishop of Melbourne. Gardenvale was in his bailiwick. Pickering was welcome company in the upper reaches of the church. He did not deny himself the finer things of life: good cars, good suits and good food. Everyone knew he drank and had a filthy temper but he put on a fine mass: lots of bells, smells, Latin and children's choirs. The choir and the altar were his hunting ground. He left a trail of wrecked kids across Melbourne. By the early 1990s they were dying. Police in Victoria have linked at least eight suicides to Pickering's crimes. Genevieve Grant, a young teacher at St James Primary School, says she tried to warn Pell in 1989 but the auxiliary bishop, visiting the school to meet confirmation students, brushed her aside and "didn't want to know." When this came to light many years later in the *Age*, Pell said: "No teacher spoke to me alleging sexual improprieties by Father Pickering on students." By this time Pickering was hiding in England from the Australian police and the Catholic Insurance Office. According to the *Age*, he fled when "a senior person in Victoria's Catholic hierarchy" tipped him off that one of his victims was about to sue. Though the Melbourne Response was compensating his victims as they came forward, the archdiocese never investigated Pickering's crimes in any systematic way. And throughout his time as archbishop, Pell sent the fugitive Pickering the monthly stipend of a retired priest. Pell told the Victorian inquiry that bishops "have an obligation to all priests who are not laicised, even if they are convicted, to continue to pay them a modest stipend. I was obliged in canon law to do that, and I did." Denis Hart took a different view. When he succeeded Pell in 2002, the payments to Pickering stopped. The priest died in England in 2009, never charged and never defrocked.

Helen Last was growing more and more concerned about the "narrow legalistic response" she saw Pell pursuing, an approach she believed put the interests of the church ahead of the needs of victims, families and parishes. She worried that Pell was not acting quickly enough. "I saw so clearly just how corrupt and twisted they were, the priests that were out there still getting away with it." Last was particularly worried that Searson was still in Doveton. "I had been aware for some time," she said, "that the southern region under Pell's jurisdiction had a very high level of abusive clergy and that Peter Searson's case had been mishandled by him as the bishop." Last says she threatened, during a meeting with O'Callaghan, that unless Searson was pulled out of Doveton she would tell the press not only about that priest but the string of criminal priests the church had sent to that parish. But Searson was in trouble again, and this time the parents had gone to the police. In October 1996 Searson bashed an altar boy over the head. His crime was to giggle during mass. A second boy gave police a statement backing the first. Pell did not move swiftly. He referred the case to O'Callaghan. Searson was not suspended until March 1997. Later that year, he pleaded guilty to the assault but "in view of the priest's unblemished record" the magistrate placed him on a good behaviour bond. Searson was never defrocked. O'Callaghan compensated a number of his victims and for eight years, out of his own pocket, supported Graeme Sleeman, the headmaster who had lost his job trying to get rid of the priest. Sleeman told the Victorian inquiry he had a call from Pell in 1996:

He said it was George Pell, and I said, "Yes George, what do you want?" He said, "What do you want?" I said, "You won't give me what I want." He said, "I don't know." I said, "I want you to go on national media and in the national printed press and say the stance that I took in Doveton was the correct one." He said, "I can't do that," and he hung up.

Last was called to Vicar-General Hart's office a couple of months after Searson's departure and told a congratulatory press release was already on its way to the media thanking her for her pioneering work in the arch-diocese. She had been fired. She was assured the priests would carry on where she left off, but the Pastoral Response Office as she knew it was soon no longer operating. When the news of her departure with full honours broke, Cudmore said: "She is a woman with a terrific knowledge of the problem, and very compassionate. There are many victims who will publicly testify to the support she gave." Pell was less generous when the *Age* called some months later: "Oh, she was alright." Last returned to private practice and is still working for victims of clergy. Her advocacy played its part in establishing the present Victorian inquiry.

Pell continued to apologise to victims, to pledge his support and meet them face to face to offer what comfort he could. Often he found himself sitting with men whose faith in the church had been completely shattered. Chris McArdle, abused as a nine-year-old altar boy in Braybrook, went to see Pell in September 1997. James Button reported in the *Age*:

> The meeting was not warm, McArdle remembers. Pell apologised to him for the past, but when McArdle asked how Pell could persuade him to return to the Catholic faith, he was amazed by the archbishop's response. "He asked me, 'Do you say the Hail Mary?'"

*

Pell's parish was the big end of town. He let Melbourne know the church was not afraid of power. He exercised his own with a freedom unimaginable to a politician. He didn't need to win hearts or votes. He had no board to please or party to keep onside. He answered only to Rome. He was the prince of Catholic Melbourne. Whatever one thought of his ambitions, he was the most effective archbishop since Mannix in his prime. Despite protests from historians, he shifted a century-old statue of Daniel O'Connell from the forecourt of St Patrick's Cathedral and put in its place an immense bronze of Mannix. Cost: $100,000. He built a mini-Vatican around the cathedral to house new church offices, a new seminary, a campus for the Australian Catholic University and the headquarters of the John Paul II Institute for Marriage and Family. Cost: $30 million. He was always a big spender. Pell brought a climate of fear to Melbourne. As books were banned, jobs lost and careers blocked, his critics became cautious. More and more they spoke to the press off the record. Pell could swat such anonymous criticism away effortlessly. He had an agenda and he got his way. If he didn't, he could become incandescent with rage. Those close to him know the volcano in George can blow at any moment. He isn't afraid to be feared. With his inner circle he is gracious, open and good company. They eat and drink well. They obey and admire him. They know that if they fall out, they won't be readmitted to his circle. Once you're out, you're out. But being camp isn't a bar to being in. The *Age* would report at the end of his reign:

> In Melbourne, the Vatican II generation speak derisively of a group of conservative younger priests they call the Spice Girls, who, they say, have been loyal Pell supporters and have acquired considerable influence in the archdiocese … "They're a bevy of younger clergy who are strongly supportive of George Pell. They're gay – I'm speaking about orientation, not practice – and they are very focused on elaborate ritual and dressing up in clerical garb, in a way that has not hitherto been typical among Australian Catholic priests.

The reports spread like wildfire. Mary Helen Woods, co-author of *Issues of Faith and Morals*, could see what they were getting at. But she told the *Sunday* program on Nine it wasn't sex, but power. "People are attracted to a powerful bloke, they tend to be a bit girlie about it and I don't mean gay, I mean girlie." For his part Pell dismissed the Spice Girl talk as an unwarranted slur: "I think it is insulting and misleading and undeserved."

Pell stood at the west door of St Patrick's in full rig in May 1999 after denying communion to fifty gay men and women, their supporters, their friends and one or two of their mothers wearing rainbow sashes. A wreath had also been laid by protesters in memory of students at Catholic schools driven to suicide by homophobia. "I haven't got good statistics on the reasons for those suicides," the archbishop told the waiting press. "If they are connected with homosexuality, it is another reason to be discouraging people going in that direction. Homosexual activity is a much greater health hazard than smoking." Correctives rained down on him from authorities on smoking, AIDS and youth suicide. Pell was unchastened. He laid the blame squarely at the door of homosexuals themselves. His logic was impeccable: if they didn't keep recruiting "new members to the subculture," there would be no gay youths to commit suicide. Pell has a fundamental faith that sexuality is malleable, that spiritual exercises can stop sex in its tracks or even change its direction. This is the ground on which he has built his commitment to celibacy, his intolerance of homosexuality, his insistence that the sex rules of Rome be obeyed and his belief (certainly at that time) that even paedophiles can be redeemed by grace and with skilled psychological assistance. The world Pell has spent his life defending is brutally simple: there is one and only one way to have sex – within marriage, open to conception – and all the rest is disobedience.

Intransigence made Pell a celebrity. Standing up to the zeitgeist, demanding obedience, listing sins and condemning sinners kept him in the news. He had expert advice on doing this. Soon after becoming archbishop, he engaged the crisis manager Royce Communications, and its CEO, Peter Mahon, has become a familiar, ginger-haired presence at Pell's side in the years since. Royce was there for the Melbourne Response, on hand for Rainbow Sash, and guided Pell during his quixotic campaign to have Andres Serrano's *Piss Christ* – a vermilion and gold photograph of a crucifix bathed in urine – removed from the walls of the National Gallery of Victoria. Royce helped the church navigate the reefs and shoals of the child abuse scandal as more victims went to the media and more paedophile priests went to prison. And if euthanasia or violence on television was the subject of the day, Pell was there with a crisp, dogmatic grab. Drug-taking? "Wrong and sinful." Original sin? "Alive and flourishing." Universal innocence? "A dangerous myth." IVF for single mothers? "We are on the verge of creating a whole new generation of stolen children." That created a most satisfying uproar. The failings of the church? "We're frightened to put forward the hard teachings of Christ."

Every five years the bishops of Australia travel in state to confer with the Vatican. At their *Ad Limina* meeting in 1998, Geoffrey Robinson tried to focus attention on clerical sex abuse: "Victims of abuse and the whole community demand that all aspects of the life of priests and religious be studied and that all attitudes to power and authority be carefully reviewed." But there was no appetite for that in the Holy City. Pat Power, another of the bishops present, told me: "They still hadn't got it in Rome." Instead the bishops were ambushed and compelled to sign a statement that blamed "the tolerance characteristic of Australian society" for encouraging Catholics on this side of the world to become indifferent to truth. The Statement of Conclusions went into the problems in Australia in great detail. On the Vatican's list were "a decline in the sense of sin," "the legitimation of homosexual relationships" and "an extreme individualism, seen especially in a concept of conscience that elevates the individual conscience to the level of an absolute." These might have been Pell's words. And there was not a line in that bulky document about clerical sex abuse. Pell was learning to use Rome to get his way in Australia. Heroin addicts were dying in the streets of Sydney and Melbourne, and the Sisters of Charity, who run St Vincent's Hospital in Sydney, were preparing to open Australia's first medically supervised injecting room. All was going well. Politicians and the church were working hand in glove. Then the Congregation for the Doctrine of the Faith issued orders in October 1999 forbidding the sisters from going ahead. Pell was in Rome for these deliberations. The congregation's decision was to have an impact far wider than one drug crisis in one city. It was Rome's signal to Catholic health organisations worldwide. They all pulled back.

John Howard welcomed the veto. The two men had come to matter a great deal to each other. Pell's oldest political loyalties were to the DLP, but when the party collapsed Santamaria had directed his followers to cross the bridge to the Liberals. It was not altogether comfortable for either party, so it mattered a great deal for Santamaria's people when Howard reconciled with the old man at the very end. Pell was at the bedside as Santamaria lay dying:

> During his last days he was paralysed on his left side, unable to speak and only able to move his right arm. But when I blessed him, he struggled successfully to make the sign of the cross. This gesture was not a poignant return home after a lifetime of wandering, it was a determined reaffirmation of the faith that inspired him through so many vicissitudes, that sustained him in defeats and victories and brought him to the God he served so well.

Howard ordered a state funeral. Two hundred priests and bishops turned out at St Patrick's. Pell did the honours. In his fine eulogy, Pell pledged himself all over again to the cause pursued by this "maddeningly" pessimistic and implacable figure who had been "the most influential Catholic voice in Australia."

Despite their alliance there were always little differences between the archbishop and the prime minister. Pell condemned brute capitalism and the "growing gulf between rich and poor." He chided Howard for trying to curtail native title rights. He blamed the appearance of One Nation on the "drastic consequences of globalisation." And he was a determined opponent of the monarchy. His fellow bishops had decided rather cautiously not to adopt a single Catholic position on the republic, but Pell powered ahead. Whether he did the cause much good is another issue. "He repels people essentially," said the Australian Republican Movement's campaign director, Greg Barns. Perhaps so, but the republican campaign helped make the archbishop of Melbourne a national figure. And it reminded the bishops once more that he was his own man.

They had called on the prime minister in 1998 not to include "the essentials of life" in his planned goods and services tax. As the elections of that year approached, Howard had ranged against him on the GST the Labor Opposition, the left of his own party and most of the churches. They were all particularly hostile to the idea of a goods and services tax on food. Supporting the bishops were institutions Pell always suspected of left-wing sympathies: St Vincent de Paul and the Catholic Social Welfare Commission. As Howard's hopes of re-election began to fade, he and his ministers lashed out at the churches. Then Pell intervened. Through Royce Communications, he put out a statement: "There is no one Catholic position on an issue as complex as taxation." Those thirteen words were a godsend for Howard. He used Pell's name all the way to polling day. "He's not taking sides," he said. "He's speaking common sense and he's saying the obvious thing. Let the individual Australian make up his or her mind as to whether this is good for their country ..." Howard scraped home. The bishops were furious. Pell had done more than break ranks this time: he had silenced them. Australians were treating this unlikely, Roman figure as the voice of the Catholic Church. Pell was unmoved. He didn't need these men. He answered elsewhere.

*

Pell loved Melbourne. It was his stage: the biggest and richest archdiocese in the nation. He knew the politicians and the politics of the city intimately. He was a member of the Melbourne Club. Information flowed to him from every corner of the town. He ran a magnificent cathedral. The place was packed. Out in the parishes attendance at mass continued to sag but Pell's faith in renewal through doctrinal purity was unshaken. One day the pruned tree would grow abundantly. More money than ever was going into the plate. The seminary had a meagre twenty-six candidates for the priesthood but had returned to a life of regulated piety. Measured in every other way but turning up on Sunday, the Catholic Church was growing. Catholic schools were teaching more children and Catholic hospitals treating more patients than ever. Pell could take a great deal of the credit for the establishment of the Australian Catholic University. A remarkable achievement: sectarian higher education funded in the late twentieth century with public money. He could say, rightly: "We're as much a part of the national conversation as we've ever been." He had done all this as archbishop of Melbourne. But Sydney was the price Pell had to pay for a cardinal's red hat.

On 26 March 2001 Rome announced his translation to Sydney. In the tide of commentary that washed him north, little was said about his handling of paedophilia in church ranks. It was not yet – not quite yet – seen as a big issue in his career. He would tell the Victorian inquiry: "I stood down plus or minus twenty priests in my five years in Melbourne." O'Donnell had gone to his grave still a priest. Efforts to defrock Baker were proving fruitless. Pell was apologising to Pickering's victims while posting monthly cheques to him in England. The work of the Melbourne Response ground on. Pell told the *Sunday Age* after its first year: "We have dealt with most of the backlog." He was completely mistaken. Victims were still queuing at O'Callaghan's door and would continue to turn up long after Pell left the city. By June 2012 O'Callaghan had accepted as proven complaints from 304 men and women of abuse by about sixty priests over eighty years.

About half those victims would tell the Victorian inquiry that for one reason or another they were highly dissatisfied with the process. So were the police, who accused O'Callaghan of referring not a single complaint to them. O'Callaghan was outraged by this. He insisted he had made every effort to encourage victims to go to the police, but documents he produced to the inquiry suggest only about ten victims went to the police *after* first seeing O'Callaghan. He produced only four examples of victims doing so with "the encouragement of or with the assistance of the independent commissioner." There were victims who found the processes of the Melbourne Response gruelling; victims furious that they had to pay their own legal bills; victims who found it painful to face their abusers. And there were complaints from victim after victim about the sums they were paid at the end of the process, sums they had to accept because the alternative was the almost impossible task of suing the church. Pell was unfazed earlier this year when he faced the inquiry and one of the parliamentarians read him the testimony of an angry victim:

> Any Australian citizen can go to a court. This is what Australia is about. It is a democratic country. I need to go there to get proper democracy. That is what I want ... I got twenty-seven grand for being bloody raped ten times, apart from all that sort of trying suicide – the whole works ...
>
> I want a proper Australian court to basically say, okay, I can go to court, and this is what happened there, and to have an Australian judge, like any other citizen within Australia is able to do that, whereas with this mob I cannot because there is some – I do not know what the hell it is or where it comes from – law that these international paedophiles can ... get away with it.

Pell conceded the compensation offer was "miserable" but defended the system that effectively locks victims out of the courts. His mantra was: "We have always complied with the law of the land, and we will comply with the law of the land in the future." The size of the cap does not trouble him. He told the inquiry: "I have acted compatibly with the general standards of the community and I have tried to be generous." The cap had been raised by 2009 to $75,000 but that modest maximum seems to have been paid rarely. The maths was laid before the inquiry: the Melbourne

Response has paid 287 victims a total of $9,319,750. The average payout is risible: about $32,500. What the victims might have won if the courts were open to them can only be guessed at: perhaps ten times as much, perhaps more. Last year the Economist did the sums for America, where the church doesn't enjoy the protection from litigation it does here: "Sexual-abuse cases typically cost the church over $1 million per victim."

The Fosters decided to sue rather than accept the $50,000 offered to their daughter Emma for her repeated rape by Father Kevin O'Donnell. The toll on them had already been appalling. Now they were made to fight every inch of the way. Despite O'Donnell's confessions and prison sentence; despite admissions to the Fosters by the Melbourne Response; despite the written apology they had received from Pell, the church now denied any "physical and/or sexual and/or psychological abuse" by the priest. The family was made to fight every inch of the way. Their lawyers compelled the church to produce documents that showed the archdiocese had known about O'Donnell's crimes for over forty years. That didn't take the Fosters over the ramparts but they had crossed the moat. Rather than risk a trial that might bring down the walls, the archdiocese of Melbourne settled with the Fosters for $750,000 plus costs after a nine-year battle. "I still don't understand," Chrissie Foster wrote, "why we were made to fight so long and hard."

One day another statue may appear in the forecourt of St Patrick's Cathedral somewhere near the mighty figure of Daniel Mannix. The rhetoric on the plinth would be difficult to draft, but the message would be that George Pell, archbishop of Melbourne, 1996 to 2001, saved his church a lot of money.

CARDINAL

A large figure in purple climbed out of a black stretch Ford. Anarchists jeered. Charismatics sang "Hallelujah." George Pell had come to be installed in his new cathedral. He was armed for trouble. On the way over he had paused at the tomb of Mary MacKillop to pray for "help and protection." She did not desert him now. Nor did the police. They arrested five members of Community Action Against Homophobia for swearing, assault and breaches of the peace. They were chanting, "Shame, Pell, shame," and waving placards that read: "Get your rosaries off our ovaries." Their target wished everyone in the forecourt of St Mary's Cathedral "without exception" his best wishes and made for the doors and the waiting trumpets. Inside, the Catholic Church was in triumphal mode: all the bishops of Australia and hundreds of priests packed onto stack-away chairs. It looked like a church without a trouble in the world. Pell made his way down the nave, moving in deliberate slow motion to the anthem "Behold a Great Priest, Who in His Days Pleased God." Present also were ranks of secular VIPs, including the prime minister and the leader of the Opposition. The apostolic nuncio presented instructions from the pope to administer his new diocese in a "vigilant and efficacious manner" in order that the people of Sydney may "demonstrate openly their love of the mother church." The old cardinal sat the new man in a large red chair and gave him a gold crook. The place filled with singing. Then Pell got down to business: calling on history, pleading for vocations, mocking Sydney's pretensions to be at the cutting edge of sin: "One or two local writers seem to suggest that sin is a recent Sydney invention; 'Sin City' or 'Tinsel Town' has a contemporary local resonance! However, human weakness flourishes in other parts of Australia and ... human perfidy is as old as the Garden of Eden."

The installation of Pell in late March 2001 marked the arrival of a big, and perhaps turbulent, civic presence. He was, however, dealing with a different town and a different church. This was not Santamaria territory.

New South Wales and its hierarchy had sided against Pell's kind of Catholic. That history wasn't forgotten. Pell didn't yet have the networks, the alliances. He threw himself into politics with familiar energy and fair success: he helped hold the line on euthanasia while losing on embryonic stem-cell research. Everything was going well. Down south, fresh news of clerical sex crimes kept breaking but in Sydney this was hardly reported. It was as if he had left the scandal behind. Walking Ridsdale to court was the only detail the public knew that touched his reputation and he had explained that slip years ago. In early 2002, when the *Boston Globe* published the first, best exposé in the world of how the Catholic Church covered for paedophile priests, Pell was frank but reassuring. The lessons had been learnt, all was well now, but there had been mistakes in the past: "For a variety of reasons — some of them half-bad, some of them bad — there's been an abuse of power by authorities who should have been more vigilant."

Pell could sit back while the Anglicans took some heat. Indeed, he joined the general clamour for the Right Reverend Peter Hollingworth to resign as governor-general for failing to take decisive action against paedophiles in Anglican ranks. "As governor-general he has to have basic support across the whole community," said Pell. "I am unsure this is now true and unsure how he can retrieve the situation." The Anglicans decided it was time to investigate the extent of paedophilia in their church, to dig down and find out how bad it was. This was never something the Catholics were keen to do. Within weeks the Anglican archbishop Phillip Aspinall had to admit a private church inquiry did not have the muscle required to carry out the investigation: "An independent, and in effect private, inquiry of this sort cannot provide protection to those who participate, nor can it compel anyone to answer questions." He could have been referring to the Melbourne Response and Towards Healing. Aspinall turned to John Howard to hold a national inquiry. The premier of Queensland, Peter Beattie, backed the archbishop's request. Pell made his opposition known. He didn't see the point of looking back, only forward.

"What we need," he said "is for all organisations, including churches, to have clear protocols." Howard rejected Aspinall's plea.

The idyll of Pell's first year in Sydney was brought to an end by prostitutes and pornographers. Weary of being denounced by Christians, they published a little booklet with a monk on the cover and a long list inside of the clerical sex fiends of the nation. When Chrissie Foster rang the Eros Foundation for more copies of *Hypocrites: Evidence and Statistics on Child Sexual Abuse amongst Church Clergy, 1990–2000*, she fell into conversation with the lobby's director, Robbie Swan. He listened to the appalling story she had to tell about the rape of her two daughters and said: "I know a producer at 60 Minutes." The introductions were made. *Sixty Minutes* began to explore attempts by the church to silence its accusers. Victims from St Alipius told their stories to camera. The Fosters – with a fake moustache on Anthony and a bad wig on Chrissie – talked of their ordeal and how the Melbourne Response had demanded confidentiality. And the producers found David Ridsdale in England, who gave his account of the phone call he made to denounce his uncle to Pell. When Pell sat down with Richard Carleton and his cameras in late May 2002, he had no idea what was about to hit him. Carleton was lethal. He treated the archbishop exactly as he would a politician: with no deference and some scorn. Pell denied responsibility for the paedophile teachers of Ballarat; denied trying to buy David Ridsdale's silence; and claimed, to the amazement of the Fosters watching the show that night, not to be able to remember that photograph of their daughter Emma with blood streaming down her arms. "I have no recollection of that," said Pell. "I mean it's an awful … I don't believe I ever saw that." And Pell denied, despite the confidentiality clause they were asked to sign, that the $50,000 offered to the Fosters by the Melbourne Response was "hush money."

> CARLETON: Why do you impose this condition, sir?
> PELL: Because many of them don't want to be subjected to publicity and of course it's shameful for the Church.

CARLETON: Archbishop, thank you.

PELL: Good, thank you.

Pell's reputation shifted on the night 60 Minutes broadcast "Loss of Faith" in June 2002. Australia saw the leading Catholic churchman of the nation depicted as hostile to victims and protective of the church. Melbourne knew something of his history with the catastrophe facing the church. Now Australia was told he had a case to answer. He went on the offensive even before the show went to air, holding a press conference – with Royce's Peter Mahon at his side – to deny trying to silence David Ridsdale and the Fosters. Every church in Sydney that Sunday distributed a statement from him repeating the denials. After Australia saw the show that night, he held a second press conference to sharpen his attack on David Ridsdale. He accused the young man of making claims that were "inconsistent, discredited and wrong." He was brilliantly insinuating. David Ridsdale fought back point by point. The story was everywhere. This is when Australia learnt about Father Ridsdale and St Alipius and the paedophile priests of Melbourne. After the reports from Boston the accusations levelled against the church had a new edge. Surely Pell must have had an inkling of what was going on in Ballarat? He maintained his absolute denials. Channel Nine conducted a couple of internet polls in the middle of this: one split roughly fifty-fifty on whether Pell should resign but the other split 84 per cent to 16 per cent in favour of holding an inquiry into "Catholic Church sex abuse claims." Once again Prime Minister Howard refused calls for a royal commission and endorsed Pell: "I've always found him to be a person of intense, of great intelligence and somebody who I respect enormously." At a cost of roughly $50,000, Pell and Archbishop Hart published full-page advertisements in city newspapers to explain the work of the Melbourne Response and Towards Healing. They pledged: "Victims are not silenced as a condition of receiving counselling or compensation."

That was a mistake. The secrecy issue was a terrible tangle. The Melbourne Response did not, technically, forbid victims to talk about their abuse but it certainly encouraged their silence. Much tougher restrictions had been imposed on victims everywhere else in Australia until December 2000, when the rules of Towards Healing were changed. That gave Pell and Hart the confidence to say the church was no longer insisting victims stay silent. But a very Catholic problem was lurking here: no one was policing the bishops to make sure the rules were applied. To the intense embarrassment of the church, victims now came forward with proof that hush money was still being paid. A story in Sydney's Sun Herald began: "A disabled woman who said she became pregnant after being raped by a Catholic priest had to sign a secrecy clause before the church would pay her $15,000 compensation." That settlement had been struck only a month earlier in rural New South Wales. A leading church barrister explained: "A bishop is not a lawyer." Pell tried to step clear of the mess out in the bush. "I am archbishop of Sydney," he told his congregation that Sunday, "not the archbishop of New South Wales."

Spending World Youth Day in Toronto with the pope and hundreds of thousands of devout Catholics must have seemed a welcome prospect for Pell after this ordeal by television. His standing with John Paul seemed higher than ever. He had been reappointed to the Pontifical Council for Justice and Peace and asked to join the Synod of Bishops. The pope had also given him a delicate assignment: to be president of Vox Clara, the committee advising the Vatican on English translations of liturgical texts. Years of difficult work lay ahead protecting orthodox rigour and Latin forms from the inroads of modern English. Within days of reaching Toronto, Pell showed his own blunt way with words. "Jesus offers punishment and consequences," he told 500 young Catholics who had gathered to hear him. "It's right through the Gospels." A visiting youth minister from Kentucky asked him how Americans should respond when questioned about sex scandals in their church. The US bishops' conference had just issued a profound mea culpa: "We are the ones who chose not to report the criminal actions of priests to the authorities, because the law did not require this. We are the ones who worried more about the possibility of scandal than in bringing about the kind of openness that helps prevent abuse." Pell's rather different tack was ridiculed around the world. He urged the young pilgrims to keep things in proportion: "Abortion is a worse moral scandal than priests sexually abusing young people."

Pell was about to enter a dark valley. As he was tangling with *60 Minutes* and declaiming in Toronto, Phillip Scott was taking first to Broken Rites and then to Towards Healing his claim that the archbishop of Sydney was "Big George" who had abused him all those years ago on Phillip Island. Nothing was said to Pell as Towards Healing tried to sort out what to do. Scott was urged to take his complaint to the police. He refused. The back and forth was brought to an end when Scott's story broke on an independent media website. Church lawyers threatened prosecution for criminal libel. The media was silent but Pell now knew what was afoot. A few days later, having absolutely denied Scott's allegations, he stood aside while Alec Southwell QC, a retired Victorian Supreme Court judge, investigated Scott's claims. John Howard did not wait for Southwell. He said at once: "I believe completely George Pell's denial."

Within hours of Pell stepping aside, the press knew his accuser had led a life of crime with the Painters and Dockers' Union and served several terms in jail. Most recently he had been in trouble for trafficking in amphetamines. Scott's name was not reported. Everything else was. The source of that leak has never been found. Peter Mahon denied it was Royce Communications. Both sides hired very able lawyers. A hunt began on both sides to find former altar boys who might be witnesses to what happened on the island in the summer of 1961 or 1962. Neither side found a witness to corroborate Scott's story nor turned up another victim to accuse Big George. Michael Foley – the boy Scott remembered telling Big George to "fuck off" before trying to burn the camp down – had followed him into a life of crime and died in a pub brawl. There was one man known only as "H" who remembered Foley warning him that year on the island: "Just watch out for Big George." Young as he was, this former altar boy "presumed there was a sexual context of the warning" and thereafter didn't "get too close" to the tall seminarian. Southwell thought "H" "patently honest" but Foley wasn't around to say what he had meant by the warning all those years ago. Southwell rejected this hearsay evidence. "Not without hesitation," said Southwell, "I have decided that, given the very serious nature of this proceeding, and possible ambiguity of the warning, I should put it aside."

The contest raged for five days in Melbourne behind closed doors in the boardroom of Rydges Hotel in Exhibition Street. Southwell was running another of the private church tribunals that appear often in this narrative: good lawyers with impeccable reputations clothed in the language of a royal commission but with none of a commissioner's powers to protect witnesses and compel production of evidence. Without witnesses for either side, the result turned on the credibility of the protagonists. Pell's credibility was unchallenged. Scott's had survived forceful attack almost unscathed. Both men had given Southwell the impression of speaking the truth. Southwell found the case for and against Pell too evenly balanced to bring down the "grave, indeed devastating" consequences of preferring Scott's complaint to Pell's response. He wrote:

> In the end, and not withstanding that impression of the complainant, bearing in mind the forensic difficulties of the defence occasioned by the very long delay, some valid criticism of the complainant's credibility, the lack of corroborative evidence and the sworn denial of the respondent, I find I am not satisfied that the complaint has been established.

Both sides welcomed that verdict delivered in mid-October 2002. Scott's solicitor said: "We have been vindicated." Pell returned to work after eight weeks in the wilderness saying, "I am grateful to God that this ordeal is over and that the inquiry has exonerated me of all allegations." He has claimed ever since that Southwell cleared him. But there were those who saw the result as more ambiguous. The *Sydney Morning Herald* pointed out that Southwell had demanded a high standard of proof akin to the "beyond reasonable doubt" of criminal proceedings: "That helped Dr Pell. It also made Mr Southwell's careful conclusion that he could not be 'satisfied that the complaint has been established' rather less than a complete exoneration."

*

The Rome of John Paul's last years was obsessed by papal power. A long reign was ending, and as the pope sank under the weight of Parkinson's disease the demands for obedience became more pressing. More than ever, the great marker of submission was devotion to the sex rules of the church. War, poverty and disease were not ignored, but the energies of Rome were poured into combating contraception, homosexuality, genetic engineering, divorce and abortion. Pell was deeply involved with this work. The Pontifical Council for the Family on which he sat produced in April 2003 a 900-page *Lexicon on Ambiguous and Colloquial Terms about Family Life and Ethical Questions*, which taught, among many strange things, that to allow homosexuals rights is to "deny a psychological problem which makes homosexuality against the social fabric." As the scandal of paedophile priests deepened in the outside world, Rome came to the view that the underlying problem was actually homosexuality. The solution was to keep homosexuals out of seminaries. The pope's spokesman, Joaquin Navarro-Valls, told the *New York Times* in 2002: "People with these inclinations just cannot be ordained." Rome, meanwhile, was rejecting the tough line on paedophiles adopted by the American bishops the same year. When he was exposed by the *Boston Globe* for covering up the crimes of his priests, Cardinal Bernard Law was brought to the Vatican and given a position of high distinction. Bureaucratic infighting in the Holy City over which of the Vatican's departments would deal with criminal priests finally ended in 2003, when the task was given to Ratzinger's Congregation for the Doctrine of the Faith. It remained Rome's jealously guarded prerogative to laicise priests. Defrocking even convicted criminals was still extraordinarily difficult.

This was the Rome Pell served in Australia. With the annus horribilis of 2002 behind him, he got to work campaigning against the "morning after" pill, Postinor-2; protecting embryos from scientists and foetuses from surgeons; denying communion to remarried divorcees; fighting calls for same-sex marriage; objecting to homosexuals being given the same age of consent as heterosexuals; defending priestly celibacy; and combating his old bête noire, personal conscience. From his perch on the Synod of Bishops, Pell was able to appoint two ultra-orthodox Melbourne colleagues as auxiliary bishops of his new hometown: Anthony Fisher and Julian Porteous. The Sydney pragmatists were appalled. It was little wonder, perhaps, that John Paul was thought to regard Pell at this time as "a model bishop." Nor was it any surprise when, from his Vatican window in September 2003, he read out Pell's name as one of thirty-one new cardinals. The appointment provoked open dissent among Australian bishops. Pat Power of Canberra-Goulburn took his future in his hands:

> Many of the values that I think are dear to Australian Catholics, such as the dignity of the human person, the primacy of conscience, the theology of communion, the need for dialogue in our church, reading the signs of the times, I don't think they're values that are particularly clearly enunciated by Archbishop Pell and I think for that reason that many people will be disappointed that the church is going further in a direction that is not really catering for their needs.

In a crowded St Peter's Square on a mild spring day later that year, a frail John Paul gave Pell his red hat. Days later Pell modestly acknowledged in his *Sunday Telegraph* column that he was now a prince of the church. He added: "The spectacular crimson vestments are to remind us that cardinals should be prepared to die in witnessing to Christ's person and teaching, as the early martyrs did in the pagan Roman empire."

From that moment speculation began that Pell was about to be called to some great office in Rome. Such talk has continued ever since. "If Pell had actually received all the Roman jobs for which he's been prominently mentioned," wrote John L. Allen Jr of the *National Catholic Reporter* a couple of years ago, "by now he would virtually be running the Vatican all by himself." Allen sees Pell as the best living example of a species of ecclesiastical life known as the "rumour magnet":

- They have Roman experience, making it reasonable to think that they might one day head a Vatican office.
- They're perceived as enjoying a close relationship with the current pope.
- They take strong positions on controversial issues, giving one camp in their local church a strong desire to see them promoted and another camp a strong desire to see them move on.
- They have a high media profile, so they're well known both inside the church and in the broader society …

Even if the rumour magnets don't wind up in a Roman post, they have already succeeded in one sense: They've engaged the public imagination more than virtually any prelate who actually has occupied a senior Vatican assignment. That, in itself, is a kind of accomplishment — and by that measure, Cardinal George Pell is virtually in a class by himself.

In 2010 word spread that Pell would soon be the fourth-most powerful man in Rome by becoming the new prefect of the Congregation for Bishops. John Paul was dead. Pell had campaigned for the election of his friend Joseph Ratzinger and the new pope was, more than ever, opening the great offices of the Vatican to non-Italians. In May, Rome's *Il Giornale* reported that Pell had the backing of Pope Benedict's secretary of state, Cardinal Tarcisio Bertone. The man whose appointments had reshaped the Australian church in the image of his old-fashioned Ballarat Catholicism would soon be choosing the bishops of the world. Everything was set. Pell was said to have chosen an apartment in the Via Rusticucci, a couple of blocks from St Peter's. But in June *Il Giornale* declared: "Everything seems to be in doubt." Pell was reported to have declined the appointment on the grounds of ill health, but that was treated by the Italian press as a diplomatic cover for this little disaster. Two problems had emerged. The first was a backstairs conspiracy to damage Pell's patron Bertone. The second was Phillip Island. Quoting *La Stampa*, the ABC's Paul Collins wrote: "The fear in the Vatican is that appointing someone to Bishops 'who had been accused in the past,' even if cleared, created the danger of a civil case still being brought against him because he was such a high-ranking church official."

*

Rome had made the old mistake of failing to understand local conditions. Any lawyer knowing the lie of the land would advise extreme caution before suing a bishop in Australia, let alone taking on the church. As a result of the Sydney archdiocese fiercely defending a case brought by John Ellis, Australia remains the only country in the common-law world where the Catholic Church cannot be sued. Ellis was no ordinary litigant. He had been a partner of Baker & McKenzie, one of the biggest law firms in the world, until he had a crack-up and lost his job. He and his doctors put his troubles down to years of sexual abuse that began when he was an altar boy at the parish of Christ the King in the western suburbs of Sydney. Ellis was thirteen when Father Aidan Duggan began taking a special interest in him. What began as coffee and Latin coaching ended in oral and anal sex. This went on for years. Soon after Ellis married for a second time, his life began to fall apart. He was anxious, angry and self-harming. He approached Towards Healing. In late 2002 he had a letter from Pell saying Duggan was now too old and demented to deal with complaints of abuse. Duggan died penniless. Ellis's life continued to slide. Towards Healing offered him $30,000. He asked for $100,000. At this point his behaviour had become so chaotic that he was sacked by Baker & McKenzie. With no job and in wretched health, he prepared to sue the church. His offer to settle for $750,000 brought no response from the church's lawyers. Many years later Pell would call that silence "unfathomable" and admit that he was, at the time, under the misapprehension that Ellis's claim was "for many millions of dollars." The decision was taken in 2005 to fight Ellis in court.

Hardball is the default setting of the church's lawyers. Speaking to the *Australian Financial Review* in 2002, Peter Gordon of Slater & Gordon, one of the big firms representing victims of clerical sexual abuse, said: "I would rank the Catholic Church in 'group one' in terms of aggression as a litigious opponent. That puts it alongside the tobacco industry and one rung above breast-implant manufacturers, asbestos companies and doctors." The church got a shock in March 2006 when the NSW Supreme Court allowed Ellis to sue the trustees of the Roman Catholic Church for the archdiocese of Sydney. This was a serious breach of the church's defences. Hitherto, the courts had always accepted the argument that the trust – which holds the assets of the church – has nothing to do with the placement, direction and discipline of priests. It looked after property and couldn't be expected to compensate the victims of paedophile clergy. The church took the case to the NSW Court of Appeal, which delivered an encyclopaedic judgment that was all the church could have hoped for. The court confirmed that priests aren't employees; that an archbishop can't be sued for the failings of his predecessors; that the trustees can't be sued for the failings of clergy; and that the church can't be sued because it's just an association of believers with no corporate identity, rather like a mothers' club or a bridge circle. Ellis was left with nothing and no one to fight. The Catholic Church and all its schools and hospitals and mighty cathedrals had disappeared into thin air. Ellis appealed to the High Court, where his barrister begged the judges to correct "an outrage to any reasonable sense of justice." But they declined, instead confirming the grim view of the court below that Ellis's bid to sue over Father Duggan's crimes was "doomed to fail." The church then demanded Ellis pay its legal costs of $755,940.

Pell and Ellis met a year later. Ellis claims the cardinal admitted the litigation was "legal abuse" and promised to do things differently in the future. The church dropped its demand for costs. So the church paid its lawyers almost exactly what it wouldn't pay Ellis. Pell boasts of the church's generosity to its defeated adversary, helping with medical and other bills. Even so, the Ellis case represented remarkable value for money: it confirmed that the immense wealth of the church is – unless the church itself decides otherwise – beyond the reach of victims of abuse. They may receive charity but they don't have rights. The financial advantage to the Catholic Church is colossal. According to an impeccable source, the church has so far paid about $100 million to victims of child abuse in Australia. But were the abusers working for other churches or state-run institutions, the payout would have been some multiples of that sum. The Melbourne Response and Towards Healing are paying, according to victims' lawyers, about ten cents for every dollar a court would award to a child abused by the clergy of another church. And victims who sue are facing hardball tactics that double the legal costs and end in as little as half the settlement they might expect from another church. It's impossible to put an exact figure on it, but the money saved by the Catholic Church in Australia runs into hundreds of millions of dollars.

The High Court may not have done with this. Superior courts in Canada and Britain have moved a long way in the last few years to make the churches more accountable to victims of abuse. They are not buying anymore the fiction that priests aren't employees. They are finding churches vicariously liable for the crimes of their priests. They are prising open property trusts. Knocking back Ellis may not mean the court is happy with the law in Australia. A shrewd observer of the High Court told me: "reading between the lines, the judges seemed to think Ellis was going to have a hard time proving his case. The claim seemed very vague. [The] Ellis [judgment] is not a brick wall. It was a bad test case. All this could be opened up again. The church is more vulnerable than Ellis suggested."

Pell says: "We have always complied with the law of the land." But that law can easily be changed. All it takes is political will. A short bill in each state parliament would place the Catholic Church on the same footing as the Anglicans, the Uniting Church and nearly every other faith in Australia. David Shoebridge of the Greens has a bill ready in the NSW parliament, but the public has yet to demand this reform. That may change. The Victorian inquiry has Ellis in its sights. And it is hard to imagine political support for the privileged immunity of the Catholic Church surviving the scrutiny of the royal commission. Meanwhile, there are many in the church too appalled to use the Ellis case to shield their assets from victims. The Jesuits don't plead Ellis. Nor did the diocese of Toowoomba under its bishop Bill Morris until 2011. "Thankfully not all dioceses take advantage of the Ellis defence," wrote Shoebridge late last year. "The Maitland-Newcastle diocese stands out, not only as having an extraordinary number of abuse claims, but also for not using the Ellis defence to defeat claims. The Sydney diocese, by contrast, takes the point every time."

*

Helicopters hovered over Randwick as the little figure of the pope climbed the long ramp to a gorgeous throng of cardinals and bishops. The day was cold and the sky threatening. Hundreds of thousands of pilgrims had kept watch all night on the racecourse. The arrival of Benedict a little after 9 a.m. provoked restrained pandemonium. Now, 3000 priests readied themselves to celebrate the last mass of World Youth Day 2008. This is as close as the church gets to the splendour that once seemed its eternal due. This is the Catholic Church George Pell went to Werribee to join. Conceived by John Paul, these events have the outward appearance of youth festivals. They are, in fact, immense acts of homage to the pope. John Paul was gone. Benedict was in Sydney. Pell was by his side. "At World Youth Day the church appears as she truly is," he said, looking out over that vast crowd of pilgrims: "alive with evangelical faith." Police were on alert to prevent the distribution of condoms. Church and state were working hand in glove to make this extravaganza a success. New South Wales and Canberra had paid all but $10 million of a bill that would run to over $140 million. But once again things hadn't gone right for Pell at World Youth Day. He was still defending his unhappy relegation of paedophilia in Toronto in 2002. Cologne 2005 had put pictures on the internet that wouldn't go away: him in an ancient cardinal's *cappa magna*, a great swathe of scarlet moire silk half a cricket pitch long held by a train-bearer. And the week before Benedict briefly turned Sydney into a holy city had been purgatory for Pell.

An angry man had taken damaging documents to the ABC's *Lateline*. Anthony Jones was in his late twenties when he had sex with Father Terrence Goodall. Abuse by priests of adults is a whole other world of bad behaviour I haven't canvassed in this essay. Jones claimed the sex was forced and sued the church. One reason the church in Australia fights to stay out of court is that trials give victims the right to demand documents. It's called discovery. All the great press stories in the United States about paedophile clerics – stories that taught the world what was really going on – came from the church's own records discovered during litigation. The documents Jones obtained and took to *Lateline* show that an investigator for Towards Healing called Howard Murray had recommended that Jones's allegations be sustained without qualification. Pell disagreed and wrote Jones a letter that misrepresented Murray's advice:

> As no other complaint of attempted sexual assault has been received against Father Goodall and he categorically denies the accusation, Mr Murray was of the opinion that the complaint of attempted aggravated sexual assault cannot be considered to have been substantiated.

That was not true of Murray's opinion or of Goodall's record. According to *Lateline*'s Conor Duffy, Pell had to know there was another serious complaint about the priest because, on the same day he wrote to Jones, "George Pell signed a letter to another man who had claimed that when he was just ten or eleven years old he'd been attacked by Father Goodall."

Pell called the press together next day and denied telling a couple of lies to fob off a victim. The letter was "badly worded," he explained, a case of "innocent error" and "overstatement" and certainly "no cover-up." Commentators were merciless. Pell shrugged off calls for his resignation. Tony Abbott offered a testimonial: "I think Cardinal Pell has a pretty good record when it comes to making sure that there is no misbehaviour on the part of the priests of the archdiocese in which he's been in charge." As so often before and since, Pell announced that a distinguished former judge – this time Bill Priestley QC – would look into the Jones case and advise Towards Healing. That advice has never been released. Later Pell would apologise to Jones and compensation would be paid. Asked at the time if the Lateline story would taint the coming celebrations, the cardinal replied: "Please God, we'll be over this before the World Youth Day."

The Fosters were in Scotland after a few days on remote St Kilda when Lateline told them about the Pell letters. They decided to return to Australia to challenge the pope and tell their story, not in disguise, as they had years before on 60 Minutes, but as themselves. Their daughter Emma had committed suicide earlier in the year. Katie had walked under a car and been left a physical and mental wreck. Anthony Foster spoke to Lateline from the ABC's London studio and the interview went to air as they were flying home. At Tokyo airport the Fosters discovered their story was being reported around the world by the press corps waiting for the pope. They were appalled to hear that Bishop Anthony Fisher, coordinator of World Youth Day, had described Anthony Foster on Lateline as "dwelling crankily, as a few people are doing, on old wounds." At Sydney airport Foster read a statement condemning Fisher and asking to meet the pope to discuss how the church might deal fairly and justly with victims, "so they may have some hope of surviving and participating fully in this wonderful gift of life." The church defended Fisher. The bishop swore he was attacking the media, not the Fosters. They bluntly contradicted him. The pope made formal apologies and later said mass in private for four victims. Barney Zwartz of the Age wrote: "The ones chosen no doubt suffered. But they were all victims who accepted the church's Towards Healing protocol, did not go through the courts and had not publicly embarrassed the church in the lead-up to World Youth Day." The Fosters never met the pope.

So Pell's round continued: half the year in Sydney and much of the rest in Rome; so many conferences and so much time in the air; so much to do and so many things to stop. Lust. Greed. A national charter of human rights. "The climate change bandwagon." Gay adoption. Lesbian adoption. The primacy of conscience. The Greens: "Sweet camouflaged poison." Ethics classes for school children. Condoms: "The idea that you can solve a great spiritual and health crisis like AIDS with a few mechanical contraptions like condoms is ridiculous." The Pill: "Below-replacement fertility." Australian Reforming Catholics. Catholic politicians who vote against the church: "It's incongruous for somebody to be a Captain Catholic one minute, saying they're as good a Catholic as the pope, then voting against the established Christian traditions." The ordination of women. Toowoomba bishop Bill Morris for advocating ordained women and married priests. "The pornification of culture." Same-sex marriage. "The progressive secularist agenda." And royal commissions into the Catholic Church.

Once it began, Pell could not prevent the fracturing of the political consensus that had protected the church for so long. Too much was happening. He had lost his great backstop, John Howard. Trials of priests and brothers continued to leach away the prestige of the church. After seven trials over fifteen years, Robert Best pleaded guilty to a last list of offences in late 2011. The trials cost the state and the Christian Brothers millions. Best had been principal of St Alipius Parish School when Pell lived next door. Once again the cardinal's Ballarat past was in the news. But the crucial political damage was done by the reports from Ireland that showed what could happen when the church was left to police itself. And they kept coming: the Ryan report in May 2009, Murphy in November 2009, Cloyne in July 2011. Ireland's church lost all its protection. In Australia reports were being written too. Philip Cummins delivered the findings of the Protecting Victoria's Vulnerable Children Inquiry in January 2012. Recommendation 48 was blunt:

A formal investigation should be conducted into the processes by which religious organisations respond to the criminal abuse of children by religious personnel within their organisations. Such an investigation should possess the powers to compel the elicitation of witness evidence and of documentary and electronic evidence.

A few weeks later Victoria Police released its report on suicides by victims of clergy abuse. A few days after that, Neil Mitchell of 3AW reduced Archbishop Hart to silence with a tough question: "Are there any priests, known by the church to be paedophiles, who are still in the community?" That got to the gap between what the church knew and what the state had been told. At the end of their difficult exchange, Mitchell asked the archbishop if he would cooperate with an inquiry into the handling of abuse cases by the Catholic Church in Victoria. He said he would. Later that day the premier announced the inquiry, to be conducted by six politicians, some Catholic and some Protestant, chosen from all parties.

Pell came to the inquiry having first done what only a cardinal can do: choose a pope. Benedict had retired and the cardinals gathered. Asked about his own chances as he left for Rome, Pell replied with great poise: "I will be coming home." This time, say Vatican insiders, Pell didn't back the winner: his man was said to be the Canadian Marc Ouellet, but the job went to Argentina's Jorge Mario Bergoglio. From those great events in that incomparable setting, Pell returned to be grilled by six politicians in a long Melbourne room hung with gasoliers in front of a gallery of press and victims and parents of victims.

No one rose when the cardinal entered. He was in civvies: black suit, white shirt, no jewellery. He took his place on one side of a long table with the politicians ranged along the other. His advisers sat nearby. "All of them," he told the committee in an awkward moment, "are married people with children, keen to help us with this fight." He had many complaints: that he hadn't been called to give evidence months ago; that he wasn't allowed to make an opening statement; that the church had

Never again miss an issue. Subscribe and save.

- ☐ **1 year subscription** (4 issues) $59 (incl. GST). Subscriptions outside Australia $89.
  All prices include postage and handling.
- ☐ **2 year subscription** (8 issues) $105 (incl. GST). Subscriptions outside Australia $165.
  All prices include postage and handling.
- ☐ Tick here to commence subscription with the current issue.

PAYMENT DETAILS I enclose a cheque/money order made out to Schwartz Media Pty Ltd.
Or please debit my credit card (MasterCard, Visa or Amex accepted).

CARD NO. ☐☐☐☐ ☐☐☐☐ ☐☐☐☐ ☐☐☐☐

EXPIRY DATE   /   CCV   AMOUNT $

CARDHOLDER'S NAME

SIGNATURE

NAME

ADDRESS

EMAIL   PHONE

tel: (03) 9486 0288 **fax:** (03) 9486 0244 **email:** subscribe@blackincbooks.com **www.quarterlyessay.com**

An inspired gift. Subscribe a friend.

- ☐ **1 year subscription** (4 issues) $59 (incl. GST). Subscriptions outside Australia $89.
  All prices include postage and handling.
- ☐ **2 year subscription** (8 issues) $105 (incl. GST). Subscriptions outside Australia $165.
  All prices include postage and handling.
- ☐ Tick here to commence subscription with the current issue.

PAYMENT DETAILS I enclose a cheque/money order made out to Schwartz Media Pty Ltd.
Or please debit my credit card (MasterCard, Visa or Amex accepted).

CARD NO. ☐☐☐☐ ☐☐☐☐ ☐☐☐☐ ☐☐☐☐

EXPIRY DATE   /   CCV   AMOUNT $

CARDHOLDER'S NAME   SIGNATURE

NAME

ADDRESS

EMAIL   PHONE

RECIPIENT'S NAME

RECIPIENT'S ADDRESS

tel: (03) 9486 0288 **fax:** (03) 9486 0244 **email:** subscribe@blackincbooks.com **www.quarterlyessay.com**

Delivery Address:
37 LANGRIDGE St
COLLINGWOOD VIC 3066

Quarterly Essay
Reply Paid 79448
COLLINGWOOD VIC 3066

No stamp required
if posted in Australia

Delivery Address:
37 LANGRIDGE St
COLLINGWOOD VIC 3066

Quarterly Essay
Reply Paid 79448
COLLINGWOOD VIC 3066

experienced "twenty-five years of intermittent hostility from the press"; that the Victorian government "was not more active earlier" investigating child abuse; and that he was so misunderstood: "I have always been on the side of victims." He never lost his temper but his colour rose all afternoon. He smiled once or twice after negotiating a difficult passage. He clasped and unclasped his hands, never quite in prayer. He droned. He snapped. At times he stared at those six politicians with a gaze focused somewhere south of Macquarie Island. The gallery was fractious but the long afternoon had gone with few interjections and only occasional bursts of laughter. No one was thrown out. The light was failing as the cardinal finished. He thanked his interrogators. "I recommit myself to lamenting the suffering and to doing what we can to improve the situation."

What was said in those four hours is the backbone of this essay. But it has taken me months to realise how baffled Pell was that afternoon. He can admit the worst: that the church hid abuse for fear of scandal and this facilitated appalling crimes. He knows children have been wrecked. He gets all that. He apologises again and again. He denounces bishops in other dioceses and other times who hid priests and destroyed documents. He acknowledges celibacy may be "a factor" in paedophile abuse. He even sees that the hostility of the press he so deplores has helped the church face the scandal. What he doesn't get is the hostility to the church. Whatever else he believes in, Pell has profound faith in the Catholic Church. He guards it with his life. Nations come and go but the church remains. What is this brief scandal compared to the history of saints and martyrs and mighty popes he first heard so long ago in his mother's kitchen in Ballarat? He is appalled, of course, by priests raping children. It was badly handled. Lessons have been learned. Reparation is being made. But this is the church: it survives unchanged and unbowed.

He is a big old man. He steps down from the altar carefully, watching his feet. In that huge bulk is at least one new hip and a pacemaker. His heart isn't the best. He leans a little on his crook. Most men of his age would be out of their game by now but, pushing seventy-two, George Pell remains eligible for the highest offices in his church. The Vatican is a gerontocracy and he is still a contender. On the nineteenth Sunday of the year, St Mary's Cathedral is respectably full. These are Pell's people: devout, not grand, some ancient skinny figures in tweed, one or two big hats and many prosperous Vietnamese families. Overhead loom several hundred thousand tonnes of Sydney sandstone and on this bright morning a power station somewhere up the Hunter is working hard to keep the place lit. The choir is magnificent. It must cost a fortune in conductors and scholarships for schoolboys, but as Pell says, casting a backward glance to his two frugal predecessors: "I am spending for three." Would but that Pell had saved on sculpture. He loves religious statues. The new stuff in St Mary's is heavy and white. Pell is exercising the prerogative of an ecclesiastical prince: art, music and ceremony.

But the tide is going out. How grim it must be for Pell to have spent his whole career watching it recede. The scandal of child abuse is not on the long list of things he blames for this. He believes it has not harmed the church at its core: only at the edges, only among those who were already drifting away. Nor does he chide himself for emptying the pews. Correction is necessary. The pruned tree will grow with renewed vigour. It just hasn't happened yet. Preaching the hard things of Christ makes him a hero on the right flank of the church – in Opus Dei and the Neo-catechumenal Way – but all his years as bishop haven't reconciled parish Catholics to his brand of Catholicism. There have always been those who see him as a careerist. The cardinal shrugs off such criticism, but David Ridsdale speaks for more Catholics than himself when he says: "Pell is a power-hungry, ladder-climbing opportunist." Except when the topic is child abuse, that sort of anger is rare these days. It was common when I began writing about Pell over a decade ago, but he's become predictable. Nothing much about him surprises Catholics anymore. They endure Pell. They say: he's Roman and that's the Roman way. Tom Keneally sees it as something deeper than that:

> He has a holding-the-line temperament. Think of those Communists who held on through everything. Some left after the famine or Hungary or Czechoslovakia. Others stayed whatever happened. It's the same in the church: people holding on no matter what. Pell is one of these, a man with a holding-the-line mentality that makes the scandals irrelevant.

Pell hasn't won over the bishops. Though he has appointed a number, they have still never elected him president of the Australian Bishops Conference. That post once came with the red hat, but not so for Pell. And in this crisis the bishops don't want him speaking for them. A few weeks after the terrible press conference Pell called to "welcome" Gillard's royal commission, the bishops set up the Truth, Justice and Healing Council, staffed with a fresh press office and new lawyers, to deal with the commission. Its chief executive officer is a layman, Francis Sullivan, with a long career in health administration for church and state. Pell hasn't been silenced. That's hardly possible. But the voice of the church has changed.

A Kyrie by Orlande de Lassus rolls down the nave as Pell sits in state. He has a heavy cold and clouds of incense set him coughing. Even so, this is as it is meant to be: a mighty sight. Pell on his throne exudes the authority he so often disavows. "I am not the Catholic prime minister of Australia," he assured the Victorian inquiry. "I am not the general manager of Australia ... my authority is limited to my archdiocese." Modesty does not become him. He is not all-powerful but there is no other church figure in this country with anything like his authority and reach. He can call Rome to his aid. He chooses bishops. Through schools, colleges, universities and hospitals he exerts influence way beyond the narrow boundaries of Sydney. He has unique leverage over religious orders, having been given a say in the fate of their valuable properties, now almost empty of monks and nuns. He keeps going for years until he gets his way. He bullies but he can also charm. His sudden acts of generosity can be disarming. Opposition to Pell is possible if kept private, but career-threatening if it spills over into the public arena. He does not hesitate to rebuke big figures in the church who cross him. He writes slashing letters. The wounds he inflicts are deep. When he puts people down, they don't get up again.

Everything that makes him a formidable figure inside the church gives him clout in the secular world beyond. He is good with people of power. They see him as one of them. He is one of the survivors of the Movement still holding to their faith in B.A. Santamaria in the church, trade unions, the opinion pages of the *Australian* and soon, it would seem, the Lodge. He and Tony Abbott have been close for a long time. Abbott is at times embarrassingly sycophantic but showed he was not Pell's puppet by giving unequivocal support to Gillard's royal commission. What a strange turn Australian politics has taken: forty years after the DLP collapsed under the weight of its own irrelevance, the Movement will have one man in the Curia and another in Canberra. Pell is about to live the dream of every prince of the church: to be spiritual adviser to a national leader.

The Gospel is read and the cardinal climbs the stairs to deliver his homily. Pell's translation of the mass is being used across the English-speaking world, but words fail him in the pulpit this morning. He can't preach. Reading Pell's sermons and newspaper columns, I was struck by how little they reveal of the man. Despite flashes here and there, his words are so shallow, so impersonal. Spiritual insight is sparse. He is intelligent, has led an extraordinary life and pursued big ambitions. Yet when he speaks there is so little there. The Gospel this morning includes Christ's difficult direction: "Sell your possessions and give to those in need." For a cardinal standing in full rig beneath the spotlights of an immense cathedral, these are challenging words. From Pell, the architect of a protocol for compensating sex abuse victims that saves the church millions, they demand deep reflection. But he just rambles. Yet at one point, reflecting on the enthusiasm for the new pope's devotion to the poor, he remarks: "Oddly enough, those clamouring for a more valid expression of poverty are often loudest in their attacks on celibacy – although surely someone who appreciates poverty (and the essential principle behind it) should be deeply sensitive to the value of celibacy."

Celibacy again. What hymns of praise this man has sung to not having sex. No sex is sacred. No sex is an offering to Christ. No sex proves our first love is to God and not one another. No sex releases energy and spirit for the service of man. No sex leaves the heart undivided. No sex makes each priest another Christ called to spiritual paternity through the sacraments. No sex means a life full of friendships. Monks brought Europe out of the Dark Ages by not having sex. Not having sex remains the distinguishing mark of holiness in a deeply sceptical world:

> The sacrifice of celibacy is still the best sign to people generally that a man is not a priest out of self-interest, while it also remains a potent witness to the reality of life after death where Christ has explained there will be no sexual intercourse.

What a relief. No struggle in heaven. But what does it do to men on earth? Most priests are part of a sexual underworld: gay, straight and at times criminal. The church has always understood that priests are human and the vow of celibacy is almost impossible to honour. The deal was that their failings would be forgiven so long as the sanctifying fiction of celibacy was maintained. Paedophilia was forgiven for a long, long time. Marriage never was. The celibate church gave paedophiles a safe haven and children. Now the damage is coming to light.

Bach, that great ecumenical spirit, thunders through the cathedral as priests, choir and liturgical extras with banners flying begin a procession to the west door. Pell is bringing up the rear. I have no reason to believe he is other than one of those rare priests who is totally celibate. But everything about him suggests he has paid a terrible price for this. He has had to gut himself to stay that way. All the rules he insists the world must follow are the rules he needs for his peculiar quest. As I read the man, listen to him and watch him in action, I wonder how much of the strange ordinariness of George Pell began fifty years ago when a robust schoolboy decided, as an act of heroic piety, to kill sex in himself. The gamble such men take is that they may live their whole lives without learning the workings of an adult heart. Their world is the church. People are shadowy. Pell is one of these: a company man of uncertain empathy. He has the consolations of friendship, music and a good cellar. And he has what inspired him from the start: a place at the highest levels of his church and a voice in the nation. He has power. His mitred head nods politely as he passes.

SOURCES

George Pell would not be interviewed for this essay. I thank his office for supplying me with documents. His biographer, Tess Livingstone, was his friendly advocate in my workroom. I had her *George Pell* by my side throughout. My colleagues in the media had been reporting Pell for over twenty years before I tried to come to grips with him. To them I have an immeasurable debt which I have tried to repay in the text and in the list of sources below. Readers will see how often I cite the *Age*: Pell was one of that paper's great subjects. My thanks to those who spoke to me on and off the record about this man and their dealings with him. Journalists know few things more inspiring than the patience of those who are willing to tell painful stories all over again. A young Melbourne lawyer, Russell Marks, was my researcher. He was a lucky find and the essay is richer for his extraordinary energy and sharp eyes.

1   "I don't think": Pell to the press conference on 13 November 2012. All quotes are from a transcript of the conference supplied by Pell's office. The audio of the conference can be found at australianpolitics.com/2012/11/13/george-pell-press-conference.html.

2   "It is not at all": Pell, *Courier-Mail*, 17 April 2002, p. 1.

2   "Ireland is not Australia": Pell, *Sydney Morning Herald*, 22 May 2009, p. 3.

2   "The revelations of the Cloyne report": Enda Kenny, 20 July 2011, www.bbc.co.uk/news/uk-northern-ireland-14224199.

3   "There is a strong public interest": Protecting Victoria's Vulnerable Children, reported in the *Age*, 1 March 2012, p. 6.

3   "It would appear": Carson, *Age*, 13 April 2012, p. 1.

3   "proactively seek" and "Victoria Police has": Submission of Victoria Police to the Parliamentary Inquiry on the Handling of Child Abuse by Religious and other Non-Government Organisations, pp. 9 and 4. www.parliament.vic.gov.au/images/stories/committees/fcdc/inquiries/57th/Child_Abuse_Inquiry/Submissions/Victoria_Police2.pdf.

4   "I have investigated": Fox, *Newcastle Herald*, 8 November 2012, p. 11.

4   "I think it needs": Pell, *Australian*, 12 November 2012, p. 2.

5   "an avalanche" and "Everyone was": *Sydney Morning Herald*, 14 November 2012, p. 5.

5   "Wherever abuse": Abbott, 12 November 2012, www.tonyabbott.com.au/Lat-estNews/PressReleases/tabid/86/articleType/ArticleView/articleId/8968/The-sexual-abuse-of-children.aspx.

5   "I will be recommending": Gillard, 12 November 2012, parlinfo.aph.gov.au/parlInfo/search/display/display.w3p;query=Id%3A%22media%2Fpressrel%2F2042400%22.

6   "The Catholic bishops": Pell's opening statement to the press conference, 13 November 2012, www.youtube.com/watch?v=pNnplUDzSZw. Otherwise, transcript as provided by Pell's office. The conference was also reported on 7.30, www.abc.net.au/7.30/content/2012/s3632078.htm, and the *Sydney Morning Herald*, 14 November 2012, p. 4.

7   "I struggle to understand": O'Farrell, 13 November 2012, www.parliament.nsw.gov.au/prod/parlment/hansart.nsf/V3Key/LA20121113029?open&refNavID=HA8_1.

8   "Everyone has to obey": Abbott, 14 November 2012, www.tonyabbott.com.au/LatestNews/InterviewTranscripts/tabid/85/articleType/ArticleView/articleId/8970/Joint-Doorstop-Interview-Brisbane.aspx.

8   Fairfax/Nielsen poll: Sydney Morning Herald, 19 November 2012, p. 1.

8   "This royal commission": Gillard, 26 June 2013, www.youtube.com/watch?v=hCJ_aavenyo.

9   "She was a woman": Pell, *Be Not Afraid: Collected Writings*, Duffy & Snellgrove, Sydney, 2004, p. 278.

10   "As a teenager": *Age*, 26 February 1998, p. 17.

10   "reasonably bright": Molony, preparation notes for "George Pell," *Compass*, ABC TV, 27 February 2000.

11   "I feared" and "no serious romances": Tess Livingstone, *George Pell*, Duffy & Snellgrove, Sydney, 2002, p. 19.

11   "He is a guy": Scarlett, preparation notes for "George Pell," *Compass*, ABC TV, 27 February 2000.

12   "He would grab": Scott, statement to the National Committee for Professional Standards, reported in the *Age*, 21 August 2002, p. 1.

12   "fuck off": Scott, in A.J. Southwell QC, *Report of an Inquiry into an Allegation of Sexual Abuse against Archbishop Pell*, 2002, p. 3.

12   "a big bastard": Southwell, p. 10.

12   "the same face": Southwell, p. 4.

12   "The allegations": *Herald Sun*, 21 August 2002, p. 1.

12   "I will stand": Scott, *Age*, 24 August 2002, p. 5.

12   "gave the impression" and "not satisfied": Southwell, p. 15.

13   "father and friend": *Advocate*, 11 June 1987, p. 7.

13   "deeply committed": Livingstone, p. 47.

13   "I came to understand": *Australian* magazine, 20 April 2002, p. 24.

14   "the principle" and "Within fifteen years": B.A. Santamaria, *Santamaria: A Memoir*, Oxford University Press, Melbourne, 1997, p. 264.

15   "an exacting man": Denis Ryan & Peter Hoysted, *Unholy Trinity: The Hunt for the Paedophile Priest Monsignor John Day*, Allen & Unwin, Sydney, 2013, p. 134.

15   "Like O'Collins": Ryan & Hoysted, pp. 134–5.

15   "another Christ": *Sunday Telegraph*, 14 May 2006, p. 78.

16   "Most of it": Ormerod to me, 30 July 2013.

16   "a fear of scandal" and "Many in the church" and "With due deference": Pell, transcript of examination by the Victorian Inquiry into the Handling of Child Abuse by Religious and Other Organisations, 27 May 2013, p. 12, www.parliament.vic.gov.au/images/stories/committees/fcdc/inquiries/57th/Child_Abuse_Inquiry/Transcripts/Catholic_Archdiocese_of_Sydney_27-May-13.pdf.

17   "Back in those days": Pell, *Australian*, 10 November 2012, p. 1.

17   "He loved swimming": Livingstone, p. 87.

17   "I was struck": Conway, *Age*, 10 April 2001, p. 13.

17   "He concealed his crimes": Pell's submission to the Victorian inquiry, p. 9, www.parliament.vic.gov.au/images/stories/committees/fcdc/inquiries/57th/Child_Abuse_Inquiry/Submissions/Cardinal_George_Pell.pdf.

18   "I wasn't the executive": Pell, "Loss of Faith," *60 Minutes*, Channel Nine, 2 June 2002.

18   "Ridsdale and Best": Walsh, *Herald Sun*, 8 June 2002, p. 19.

18   "While speaking to victims": Carson, *Age*, 13 April 2012, p. 1.

19   "I said, 'You should really'" and other quotes by Green: to me, 4 July 2013.

19   "At a distance": Pell, *Age*, 22 June 2002, p. 3.

20   "a few small changes": Livingstone, p. 127.

20   "The majority of the staff": Livingstone, p. 146.

21   "Others do the choosing": Livingstone, p. 147.

22   "enough pomp" and "high priesthood": *Age*, 22 May 1987, p. 3.

22   "We didn't want to begin": Bencomo, *Times of Arcadia*, 23 May 1985.

23   The following are from the *Protocol for Dealing with Allegations of Criminal Behaviour*, April 1992: "obstruct or pervert": paragraph 4.1.2; "such spiritual and psychological": paragraph 9.2; "that the accused": paragraph 7; "psychological therapy": paragraphs 9.8 and 9.10; "The minimisation of scandal": paragraph 9.7.1.

23   "an active, resolute" and "not merely": Santamaria, pp. 303 and 304.

24   The following are from *AD 2000*: "a spirit of hatred": November 1995, p. 17;

"enjoying a real wallow": August 1993, p. 8; "the widely publicised": September 1996, p. 2.

24 "Auxiliary bishops are responsible": Pell's examination by the Victorian inquiry, p. 32.

24 "As an auxiliary": Pell's submission to the Victorian inquiry, p. 2.

25 "He never raised": Pell's examination by the Victorian inquiry, p. 13.

25 "I suppose the archdiocesan" etc: Rafferty's examination by the Victorian inquiry, 23 January 2013, www.parliament.vic.gov.au/images/stories/committees/fcdc/inquiries/57th/Child_Abuse_Inquiry/Transcripts/Carmel_Rafferty_23-Jan-13.pdf.

26 "It was obvious": O'Donnell's examination by the Victorian inquiry, 23 January 2013, www.parliament.vic.gov.au/images/stories/committees/fcdc/inquiries/57th/Child_Abuse_Inquiry/Transcripts/Phil_ODonnell_23-Jan-13.pdf.

26 "I was on a fishing": Sleeman, *Age*, 17 September 2012, p. 1.

26 "When Searson was appointed" etc: Sleeman's examination by the Victorian inquiry, 23 January 2013, www.parliament.vic.gov.au/images/stories/committees/fcdc/inquiries/57th/Child_Abuse_Inquiry/Transcripts/Graeme_Sleeman_23-Jan-13.pdf.

28 "that Searson was extremely" etc: Pell's examination by the Victorian inquiry.

29 "objectively disordered" and "in order to protect": Congregation for the Doctrine of the Faith, *Some Considerations Concerning the Response to Legislative Proposals on the Non-discrimination of Homosexual Persons*, 24 July 1992, paragraph 12, www.vatican.va/roman_curia/congregations/cfaith/documents/rc_con_cfaith_doc_19920724_homosexual-persons_en.html.

30 "the ridicule of public opinion": Letter of His Holiness John Paul II to the Bishops of the United States of America, 11 June 1993, www.vatican.va/holy_father/john_paul_ii/letters/1993/documents/hf_jp-ii_let_19930611_vescovi-usa_en.html.

30 "Certainly his role": *AD 2000*, November 1995, p. 3.

31 All the following are from *AD 2000*: "drugs, pornography": October 1989, p. 11; "theological confusion": October 1991, p. 10; "too much sugar" and "the spread": October 1991, p. 10; "popular religious soapie", "the soft nihilism" and "King Herod's": November 1995, pp. 10–11; "However inauspicious": December 1989 – January 1990, p. 19.

31 "If you compare": Parkinson's examination by the Victorian inquiry, 19 October 2012, p. 2, www.parliament.vic.gov.au/images/stories/committees/fcdc/inquiries/57th/Child_Abuse_Inquiry/Transcripts/Prof_Patrick_Parkinson_19-Oct-12.pdf.

32   "The tone": *Sunday Age*, 15 August 1993, p. 13.

32   "commissioned a psychiatric": *OutRage*, April 1997, p. 48.

32   "Mulkearns replied": report of Operation Arcadia, reported in the *Courier-Mail*, 6 June 2002, p. 8.

33   "He was seen as a congenial" and "He would appear": *Sunday Age*, 27 November 1994, p. 2.

33   "Come here and give": *OutRage*, p. 53.

34   "He said he was" and "But nobody" and "I was afraid" and "Did you know": David Ridsdale to me, 17 July 2013.

34   "His reaction" and "all of a sudden" and "it changed everything" and "to make it" and "the bastard" and "I was actually": David Ridsdale to Richard Carleton, "Loss of Faith," *60 Minutes*.

34   "David, you have" and "an offer of help": *Age*, 8 June 2002, p. 2.

35   "When I received": Pell, media statement, 30 May 2002.

36   "a gesture of support": *Australian*, 26 July 1996, p. 11.

36   "cold comfort" and "to hold": *Sunday Age*, 15 August 1993, p. 13.

37   "He sat there" and the following quotes from Last: to me, 7 July 2013.

38   "We must live": *Age*, 10 February 1996, p. 1.

39   "Will I start": *Herald Sun*, 18 July 1996, p. 2.

39   "It is quite": *Sydney Morning Herald*, 18 July 1996, p. 5.

40   "He should have known": *Herald Sun*, 25 July 1996, p. 2.

41   "I was a junior": *Australian*, 26 July 1996, p. 11.

41   "It's a matter": *Australian*, 26 July 1996, p. 5.

41   "If you don't fix it": *Age*, 14 November 2012, p. 1.

41   "hurts and wounds," "The very worst," "It is universally," "disproportionate and repetitious," "legal games," "spotty," "If we believe" and "We are going": *Age*, 10 August 1996, p. 17.

41   "If a priest comes": *Herald Sun*, 29 October 1996, p. 19.

41   "The great majority": *AD 2000*, September 1996, p. 3.

42   "Priests, religious and church": Neil Ormerod in *Violating Trust: Professional Sexual Abuse*, proceedings of the first Australian and New Zealand Conference on Sexual Exploitation by Health Professionals, Psychotherapists and Clergy, held in Sydney, April 1996, edited by Christina Boeckenhauer, p. 191.

42   "People think": information to me.

42   "You are going to have": Pell, *Be Not Afraid*, p. 232.

43   "He made the suggestion": Pell's examination by the Victorian inquiry, p. 16.

43   "On behalf of the Catholic Church" and "a crude package": *Age*, 31 October 1996, p. 3.

43   "problems in later life": *Age*, 2 November 1996, p. 32.

43   "in relation to": Melbourne Response, Application for Compensation Form, paragraph (d).

44   "a realistic alternative": Pell's examination by the Victorian inquiry, p. 18.

44   "That was reflected": O'Callaghan's examination by the Victorian inquiry, p. 6.

44   "He was going his way": Power to me, 3 August 2013.

44   "In light of the urgent": Pell's submission to the Victorian inquiry, p. 3.

45   "to pray better": *Sunday Herald Sun*, 17 November 1996, p. 3.

45   "This book is written": George Pell with Mary Helen Woods, *Issues of Faith and Morals*, Oxford University Press, Melbourne, 1996, p. xiv.

46   "You should never": Chrissie Foster with Paul Kennedy, *Hell on the Way to Heaven*, Random House, Sydney, 2011, p. 248.

46   "A nun who had counselled": *Age*, 4 May 2002, p. 1.

47   The discussion in the presbytery: all quotes from *Hell on the Way to Heaven*: "gruelling and unpleasant": p. 158; "When Anthony mentioned": p. 159; "Anthony gave him": p. 161.

48   "No matter what I said": Pell's submission to the Victorian inquiry, p. 8.

48   Accounts of the Oakleigh meeting: these quotations are taken from the document prepared by Terry Kearney and Margaret Shields and otherwise, where indicated, from Hell on the Way to Heaven: "It's all gossip until it's proven", p. 167; "So the meeting", p. 172.

52   "I was not keen": Pell's examination by the Victorian inquiry, p. 38.

52   "He was a great": Last to me, 7 July 2013.

52   "Monsignor Cudmore's files": James O'Farrell, Director of Communications for the Catholic Archdiocese to me, 23 August 2013.

53   "There had been multiple": O'Donnell's examination by the Victorian inquiry, p. 4.

53   "despicable": *Age*, 4 May 2002, p. 1.

53   "only rumour": *Sunday Herald Sun*, 15 June 1997, p. 7.

53   "This leads me": Hart's examination by the Victorian inquiry, 20 May 2013, p. 38, www.parliament.vic.gov.au/images/stories/committees/fcdc/inquiries/ 57th/Child_Abuse_Inquiry/Transcripts/Catholic_Archdiocese_of_ Melbourne_20-May-13.pdf.

54   "If I had known": Pell's examination by the Victorian inquiry, p. 42.

54   "didn't want to know" and "No teacher spoke to me": *Sunday Age*, 31 March 2002, p. 5.

54   "a senior person": *Age*, 23 July 2012, p. 1.

55   "have an obligation": Pell's examination by the Victorian inquiry, p. 40.

55   "narrow legalistic": *Age*, 8 November 1997, p. 4.

55   "I saw so clearly": Last to me, 7 July 2013.

55   "in view of the priest's": *Dandenong and District Examiner*, 9 December 1997, p. 19.

56   "He said it was George": Sleeman's examination by the Victorian inquiry, p. 6.

56   "She is a woman" and "Oh, she was alright": *Age*, 8 November 1997, p. 4.

56   "The meeting was not": *Age*, 8 November 1997, p. 4.

57   "In Melbourne": *Age*, 31 March 2001, p. 1.

58   "People are attracted" and "I think it is insulting": *Australian*, 14 May 2001, p. 5.

58   "I haven't got good": *Age*, 24 May 1999, p. 5.

58   "new members to the subculture": *Age*, 28 May 1999, p. 15.

59   "Wrong and sinful" and "We're frightened": *Sydney Morning Herald*, 31 March 2001, p. 29.

59   "Alive and flourishing" and "A dangerous myth": *Sunday Age*, 16 May 1999, p. 24.

59   "We are on the verge": *Australian Financial Review*, 29 July 2000, p. 6.

59   "Victims of abuse": *Sydney Morning Herald*, 5 December 1998, News Review, p. 39.

59   "They still": Power to me, 3 August 2013.

59   "the tolerance characteristic" and "the loss of confidence": Statement of Conclusions, paragraph 4; "a decline": paragraph 44; "the legitimation": paragraph 7; "an extreme": paragraph 6, www.vatican.va/roman_curia/congregations/ccdds/documents/rc_con_ccdds_doc_20000630_dichiarazione-vescovi-australiani%20_lt.html.

60   "During his last" and "maddeningly" and "the most influential": *Age*, 26 February 1998, p. 17.

60   "growing gulf": *Herald Sun*, 10 June 1998, p. 27.

60   "drastic consequences": *Age*, 6 July 1998, p. 11.

61   "He repels people": *Sydney Morning Herald*, 31 March 2001, p. 29.

61   "essentials of life": *Sydney Morning Herald*, 25 August 1998, p. 15.

61   "There is no one": *Australian*, 21 August 1998, p. 1.

61   "He's not taking sides": *Age*, 22 August 1998, p. 6.

62   "We're as much": *Australian*, 30 March 2002, p. 19.

62   "I stood down": Pell's examination by the Victorian inquiry, p. 43.

62   "We have dealt": *Sunday Age*, 12 April 1998, p. 13.

63   "the encouragement": Attachment 1A to O'Callaghan's submission in reply to the police submission and evidence to the Victorian inquiry. The figures cited are on p. 3 of the submission in reply itself, www.parliament.vic.gov.au/images/stories/committees/fcdc/inquiries/57th/Child_Abuse_Inquiry/Right_of_Reply/Right_of_Reply_P._OCallaghan_Part_1.pdf.

63 "Any Australian citizen": Pell's examination by the Victorian inquiry, p. 56.

63 "miserable": Pell's examination by the Victorian inquiry, p. 57.

63 "I have acted": Pell's examination by the Victorian inquiry, p. 16.

64 "Sexual-abuse cases": *Economist*, 18 August 2012, p. 19.

64 "physical and/or sexual": *Hell on the Way to Heaven*, p. 310; "I still don't": p. 314.

65 "help and protection," demonstrators' slogans, Pell's response and nuncio's instructions: *Sydney Morning Herald*, 11 May 2001, p. 1.

65 "One or two": Pell, *Be Not Afraid*, p. 241.

66 "For a variety of reasons": *Sunday Telegraph*, 5 May 2002, p. 93.

66 "As governor-general": *Herald Sun*, 23 February 2002, p. 5.

66 "An independent": *Canberra Times*, 17 April 2002, p. 3.

67 "What we need:" *Courier-Mail*, 17 April 2002, p. 1.

67 "I know a producer": Foster to me, 18 August 2013.

67 "I have no recollection" and other exchanges: "Loss of Faith," *60 Minutes*.

68 "inconsistent, discredited": *Age*, 8 June 2002, p. 2.

68 "Catholic Church sex abuse": Livingstone, pp. 410–11.

68 "I've always found him": *Herald Sun*, 6 June 2002, p. 10.

68 "Victims are not": *Age*, 8 June 2002, p. 23.

69 "A disabled woman": *Sun Herald*, 9 June 2002, p. 4.

69 "A bishop is not" and "I am archbishop": *Age*, 10 June 2002, p. 1.

69 "Jesus offers punishment": *Globe and Mail*, 25 July 2002.

69 "We are the ones": Muriel Porter, *Sex, Power and the Clergy*, Hardie Grant Books, Melbourne, 2003, p. 55.

70 "Abortion is a worse": *Globe and Mail*, 24 July 2002.

70 "I believe completely": *Age*, 21 August 2002, p. 1.

70 "fuck off": Southwell, p. 4.

70 "Just watch out" and further evidence by "H": Southwell, p. 8.

71 "patently honest": Southwell, p. 7.

71 "Not without hesitation": Southwell, p. 8.

71 "In the end": Southwell, p. 15.

71 "We have been" and "I am grateful": *Age*, 15 October 2002, p. 9.

72 "That helped Dr Pell": *Sydney Morning Herald*, 16 October 2002, p. 16.

72 "deny a psychological": *Sydney Morning Herald*, 2 April 2003, p. 6.

72 "People with these inclinations": *New York Times*, 3 March 2002, p. 30.

73 "a model bishop": *Australian*, 23 August 2003, p. 2.

73 "Many of the values": *Sydney Morning Herald*, 30 September 2003, p. 13.

73 "The spectacular crimson": *Sunday Telegraph*, 26 October 2003, p. 52.

73 "If Pell had actually": *National Catholic Reporter*, 6 February 2010, ncronline.org/

blogs/ncr-today/australias-pell-tops-chart-rumor-magnet.

75 "The fear in the Vatican": Catholica, 13 June 2010, www.catholica.com.au/
    breakingnews/031_bn_print.php.

75 "unfathomable" and "for many millions": Letter from Father John Usher to
    Ellis, 6 August 2009, www.parliament.vic.gov.au/images/stories/committees/
    fcdc/inquiries/57th/Child_Abuse_Inquiry/Right_of_Reply/John_Ellis_
    Appendix_B_C__D.pdf

76 "I would rank": Australian Financial Review, 8 June 2002, p. 25.

76 "an outrage": Ellis v. Trustees of the Roman Catholic Church, transcript of special leave
    proceedings, 16 November 2007.

76 "doomed to fail": Trustees of the Roman Catholic Church v. Ellis & Anor, [2007] NSWCA
    117, Mason J at par. 9.

76 "legal abuse": Ellis's submission to the Victorian inquiry, 5 June 2013, p. 6,
    www.parliament.vic.gov.au/images/stories/committees/fcdc/inquiries/57th/
    Child_Abuse_Inquiry/Right_of_Reply/John_Ellis_Right_of_Reply.pdf.

77 "We have always": Pell's examination by the Victorian inquiry, p. 26.

78 "Thankfully not all": Newcastle Herald, 7 December 2012, p. 11.

78 "At World Youth Day": Sydney Morning Herald, 21 July 2008, p. 1.

79 "As no other complaint" and "George Pell signed": Lateline, ABC TV, 7 July
    2008, www.abc.net.au/lateline/content/2008/s2297016.htm.

79 "badly worded" etc: Age, 9 July 2008, p. 5.

80 "I think Cardinal": Herald Sun, 11 July 2008, p. 5.

80 "Please God": Australian, 15 July 2008, p. 4.

80 "dwelling crankily": Sydney Morning Herald, 17 July 2008, p. 6.

80 "The ones chosen": Age, 22 July 2008, p. 11.

81 "The climate change": Sunday Telegraph, 20 April 2008, p. 85.

81 "Sweet camouflaged": Sunday Telegraph, 8 August 2010, p. 45.

81 "The idea that": Sydney Morning Herald, 11 April 2009, p. 4.

81 "Below-replacement": Sunday Telegraph, 20 November 2011, p. 100.

81 "It's incongruous": Sunday Telegraph, 2 January 2011, p.5.

81 "The pornification": Sunday Telegraph, 1 June 2008, p. 88.

81 "The progressive": Sydney Morning Herald, 24 January 2006, p. 13.

82 "A formal investigation": Report of the Protecting Victoria's Vulnerable Children Inquiry, Vol.
    1, recommendation 48, p. vii.

82 "Are there any": Newcastle Herald, 1 May 2012, p. 11.

82 "I will be coming": Age, 13 February 2013, p. 4.

82 "All of them are married": Pell's examination by the Victorian inquiry, p. 2;
    "twenty-five years", p. 4; "was not more active", p. 45; "I have always", p. 4; "I

recommit myself", p. 58; "a factor", p. 4.

84   "spending for three": source to me.

84   "Pell is a power-hungry": Ridsdale to me, 13 July 2013.

85   "He has a holding-the-line": Keneally to me, 26 August 2013.

85   "I am not the Catholic": Pell's examination by the Victorian inquiry, p. 2.

86   "Sell your possessions": Luke 12:32.

87   "Oddly enough": "Homily for Nineteenth Sunday in Ordinary Time," 11 August 2013.

87   "The sacrifice": Sunday Telegraph, 14 May 2006, p. 78.

Rebecca Huntley

Anna Goldsworthy has written an engaging, humorous and elegant commentary on gender, power and the body. And yet I feel her argument leaves important issues unexplored and pays too much attention to topics that have already been well examined by others.

Goldsworthy rightly turns her attention to Gillard's now famous misogyny speech. Her analysis is terrific, but it's disappointing that she doesn't explore further how people outside the small circle of journalism and politics responded to it. If mothers did indeed show it to their daughters, it would have been useful to interview those mothers and daughters and find out what they took from it. In the social media circles I inhabit, the speech provoked a cathartic roar, connecting with every woman out there (me included) who has had to put up with a lifetime of stupid little jokes, assumptions and condescending observations from men about our capacities and aspirations. In the public opinion research I conduct, the misogyny speech triggered something more like a whisper, but nevertheless its message was heard. Women were impressed by Gillard's finely honed anger, by the way she stood up and let her opponent have it. Perhaps a part of Gillard wanted to turn around and point her finger at some of the men behind her as well? Goldsworthy observes that the discussion around the speech from sections of the media and politics was off the mark. Gillard didn't blame the problems of her leadership on sexism, but how could she ignore the different treatment? The hypocrisy of her opponent? She was, as Goldsworthy rightly says, a flawed leader, who had also to contend with sexism and misogyny.

Further into the essay, I actually clapped on reading Goldsworthy's analysis of the way Gina Rinehart was discussed on Q&A. Gillard, the most powerful person in Australia, and Rinehart, the richest person in Australia, both women, both ridiculed for being apparently ugly and unfuckable. Shame.

Once her Quarterly Essay veers away from Australian soil, Goldsworthy loses focus. I wanted more on Gillard and what the reaction to her persona and leadership reveals about the position of women here. By contrast, the observations on gonzo porn, Hilary Mantel, SlutWalks, *Fifty Shades*, *Girls* etc., albeit interesting, feel like well-traversed territory, and the connections between these topics sometimes tenuous.

Goldsworthy's greatest contribution lies in her notion that women – regardless of background or context – are required to just get on with it. She asks whether this particular brand of female stoicism masks complicity. I believe it does. "Getting on with it" is everywhere in the conversations I witness among women. This is particularly so when it comes to unpaid work in the home, where women, regardless of their employment status, continue to occupy a second-class role and seem to feel there is nothing to be done about that. Women constantly complain of their partner's lack of responsibility and responsiveness when it comes to maintaining the home and the family, and about the endless to-do list generated by wife-work. The solution? Don't confront your partner about the unequal distribution of labour; it will only lead to an argument. Just get on with it. Or hire someone else to get on with it, almost certainly another woman. Goldsworthy could have done much more with this fertile theme of female stoicism, its allures and its traps.

As a social researcher I have often been asked: are Australians sexist? Does the treatment of Gillard reflect a deep vein of sexism and misogyny? In the research groups I conducted during her time as prime minister, participants were rarely as appallingly sexist as the politicians and media types who claim to speak for them. While the odd sexist comment was made, there was not the avalanche of hate you see on social media. Maybe that's because I was there, but then again my presence rarely stops racist tirades and other obscenities. Maybe it's because we can be our true selves in the digital sphere. Was that hate there, hidden as I sat in people's living rooms? I don't think so. Twitter is not the public. I tend to think the general public was better on this issue, less judgmental of Gillard as a woman leader, than the Alan Joneses and Bill Heffernans of this world.

That's not to say Gillard was treated fairly. The combination of the way she became prime minister the first time (as part of a coup that was badly timed and based on a shallow understanding of the electorate's view of Kevin Rudd) and the second time (in the aftermath of a pitiful election campaign as a result of a deal with independents) practically ensured her unpopularity. That had little to do with her gender. The mistakes she made had little to do with it either. But there is no doubt in my mind that at times she was punished more fiercely than a man, or than if she had attained power differently. In the end some just couldn't stomach Gillard's naked ambition. Naked ambition is more unsettling in a woman than a man. The expectations of our gender – that we are supposed to get what we want demurely, and to wield power from behind the throne – are still there, still strong. We are not free of such constraints on women's power.

In addition, there is a certain naivety to the assertions that Gillard was not treated badly as a woman leader, and that sexism isn't alive and well in this country. We sorely want to believe that while there might be sexist people in Australia, we are not a sexist nation. No attempt is made to articulate the distinction. We remain wedded to the concept that we are an egalitarian society where everyone is given a fair go – indeed, so wedded that to suggest otherwise elicits a hysterical reaction in some quarters. To suggest otherwise is almost to be unpatriotic.

In the end, I see what happened to Gillard's leadership less as a problem for women in power and more as a problem with a certain type of Labor man. A Labor man like Rudd, who once seemed (apparently no longer) incapable of being a team player (something women are socially conditioned to do). Labor men like the ones who orchestrated the first coup based on a poor understanding of the public mood and with so little political judgment about its impact. The Labor men who ran the 2010 campaign and the ones who undermined it. There's your gender problem. And yet, as Goldsworthy points out, the actions of a few men are rarely taken to represent the qualities and capacities of their gender. If we are looking for those who can destroy the joint, look no further than the cloistered hacks that run parts of the labour movement.

Goldsworthy is right. We are not done with feminism yet. But, as Gillard reminded us in her speech as ousted PM, it will get better.

Rebecca Huntley

Michaela McGuire

On a Wednesday night at the end of June, three weeks after Anna Goldsworthy's
Quarterly Essay was published, a freshly deposed prime minister offered more
insight into the problems that plagued her term in office than three years of
opinion pieces and editorials combined. "The reaction to being the first female
prime minister does not explain everything about my time in the prime ministership, nor does it explain nothing about my prime ministership," Julia Gillard
said, before imploring the nation to "think in a sophisticated way about those
shades of grey."

Anna Goldsworthy pre-empted Gillard's plea by offering up a nuanced, judi-
cious and, yes, sophisticated discussion of the unfinished business of women.
Goldsworthy's love of language is evident in her beautiful sentences and her
careful unpacking of the language of feminism, misogyny and sexism. She sup-
plies the newly expanded definition of misogyny and questions its effect upon
Gillard's prime ministership: "Is it possible that she may indeed be a flawed
leader, who has additionally had to contend with misogyny?" In other words,
while it does not explain everything ...

Goldsworthy wonders whether, in the months that followed Gillard's earlier
famed speech, our eagerness to brand clumsy instances of sexism as *misogynist*
– something darker and more sinister than simple sexism – might have done
feminism a disservice. "What word do we reach for when we encounter the
genuine misogynist?" she asks. It's something I've often wondered, and never
more so than when Tony Abbott or Alan Jones or Kyle Sandilands makes
another ill-considered remark about women's bodies or their rightful place.
This generation of feminists' call to arms – the endless proliferation of hashtags
on social media – has always made me cringe. In the race to decry loudly what
are often the most mundane of slip-ups, few pause to consider what has actually been said and what it actually means. By distinguishing between true

misogyny and "reflexive sexism, experienced as category error rather than gynaecological loathing," Goldsworthy has started an important conversation, but it's unlikely to be a popular one. She notes, "It is a truism that feminists are very good at telling other feminists what they should think – almost as good as men. There is an implicit moral vanity in this: *my feminism is better than your feminism, or even my feminism is the one true Feminism.*" And I wonder, will Goldsworthy find herself being told what she should think?

I've no doubt some will be quick to note that Goldsworthy has not spoken enough of the effects of sex and misogyny on non-white women, poor women, uneducated women. In not presenting an all-encompassing argument, Goldsworthy may well be rebuked for failing to do her subject justice, but as she notes in her essay, "insisting that any feminist must speak for all women is a great way to shut feminist conversation down." Goldsworthy has done an excellent job of opening up the conversation. When I was younger and more stupid, I shied away instinctively from feminism, having encountered it only in its angriest and most inflexible forms. If these were feminists, I wanted nothing to do with them. It was years before I learned that feminism is, as Goldsworthy says, a broad church. She has no intention of telling others what to think and simply presents her evidence about the wider culture of sexism, feminism and misogyny, then backs away quietly, leaving ample space for the reader to develop their own views. Goldsworthy notes that if a mother is looking to equip her daughter with tools for life, a good starting point might be Gillard's misogyny speech. I'd argue *Unfinished Business* would be a better one.

Michaela McGuire

Rachel Nolan

I'm no fool, I'm a feminist, and given that I've founded a women's organisation, been elected as a young woman MP, worked as Clare Martin's press secretary and served in the cabinet of Anna Bligh, I reckon I've done the hard yards for the feminist cause. Still, I can't immediately see how Anna Goldsworthy's essay Unfinished Business has much to do with me or with other women I know. Call me presumptuous, but I think that signifies a problem for me, the author and the women's movement per se.

Goldsworthy's argument is that Julia Gillard was the victim not just of sexism, but of outright, old-fashioned, woman-hating misogyny. To prove this, she cites Alan Jones's use of the concept of shame (with all its witch-burning, original sin, body-hating connotations), Tony Abbott's constant refrain that Gillard should "make an honest woman of herself" and Larry Pickering (remember him?!), who drew Gillard with a strap-on as Bob Brown's bitch.

Goldsworthy says the drift into misogyny is a broader social trend clearly demonstrated in pornography – the ultimate subtext of our society – which in thirty years has moved from focusing on the woman's orgasm to depicting scenes of women's subjugation and oftentimes downright abuse.

Righto.

Goldsworthy has a point, but does it really take an exploration of multiple-penetration porn scenes to make the case for feminism – the most mainstream of all social movements? That this is fairly common feminist thinking demonstrates to me how off-course the women's movement has run. At best, the argument's very academic. At worst, it's a bit weird.

Since Goldsworthy wrote her essay, we've seen Gillard's prime ministership end, and we've heard her call for a calm debate about the role of gender in all of this. She said that she didn't think sexism explained all of her experience, but that it did explain some of it.

The reason that Gillard's defeat matters – apart from the obvious point that we rolled our first woman PM in a cloud of nasty words and deeds – is that it coincides with a trend among young women to reject feminism. Between misogyny and apathy, there's reason to think that women's progress may not be assured – that we may have hit a wall or may even be going backwards.

So let's have Gillard's measured debate. After more than a decade living and working at the forefront of women's advance into political power, I agree with Goldsworthy that we're now seeing misogynists who've been let off the leash. While it's undoubtedly the case that deeply sexist and misogynistic views existed before, they were rarely expressed and to hear them now is shocking.

Coming from Ipswich, in Pauline Hanson's old seat, I find the parallel quite stark between what's happening now with sexism and the way Pauline Hanson briefly legitimised racism in the late 1990s – so too the way Tony Abbott has taken advantage of the turn, just as John Howard did when he mollycoddled One Nation.

The parallels may provide plenty of ground for feminist or general leftist out-rage, but just as racism was put back in its box by the weight of better public opinion, we are seeing the same happen to misogyny. Whether it's abusive porn or Alan Jones saying that "women are wrecking the joint," this nasty stuff shriv-els in the light of day. The process whereby the dark underbelly emerges, only to be shunned by popular opinion, with protagonists being described variously as "devos" or "relics," should be taken not as a sign of defeat by feminists, but as a clear-cut win. Misogyny is not on.

The more pertinent issue in my view is the one raised by Eva Cox. Tucked away in Goldsworthy's essay is Cox's comment that second-wave feminism "changed the structures but didn't actually change the culture." She is spot-on. Thirty years after the Sex Discrimination Act was passed (in 1984), women aren't equal in Australia's public, economic or cultural life. For that, three pos-sible reasons exist:

- women aren't up to being equal;
- they don't want equality; or
- they try for equality but face subtle barriers – *cultural sexism* – holding them back.

The first view is illegal and wrong, but the next two are very much in play. Plenty of women step back in their professional lives rather than juggle the well-nigh impossible demands involved in "having it all." Others knock themselves out at work but encounter subtle barriers, such as the tendency of male bosses to replicate themselves. When the women who choose to step back do so because they still do most of the work at home, the latter two reasons – "choice" and cultural sexism – are merged.

When I look back on the time I spent in politics, I remember instances of sexism. There was the feeling of invisibility in meetings where I'd express a point and be ignored, only for a man to be complimented later for expressing exactly the same view. There were the questions of legitimacy: when people disagreed with me (which, of course, happens publicly in politics), the tone would sometimes drift from "She's wrong" to "What the hell is this girl doing here?" And there was the downright sexism, from the local paper drawing me as a girl with pigtails and a skipping rope, to a News Limited columnist describing me as "gloriously dizzy." There were constant lesbian rumours because I wasn't married, LNP "dirt files" criticising my clothes, and an organisation – run by women – that decided I shouldn't have a say on the location of a school in my electorate because I didn't have kids. (Make no mistake, you get no extra stock of votes for being part of the sisterhood.) The sexism reached a crescendo as Anna Bligh's government neared its end. We didn't lose because of sexism, but, as was the case for Gillard, there was a nasty edge to things that made a bad situation worse.

Politics is like normal life on steroids. My experiences were public, but most working women, particularly at senior levels, will relate to them. Usual, too, was my reaction. Never once did I call sexism out, because I didn't feel sufficiently confident in myself and my position; because I knew many people would be totally blind to it; because the risk of being seen to make excuses is huge; and because the culture says it's just part of things – get on with it, don't be soft.

In her terrific book *Lean In*, Sheryl Sandberg cites research suggesting that women tend to be liked less as they gain more power, which doesn't happen for men. The British researchers Michelle Ryan and Alex Haslam have demonstrated a "glass cliff": a tendency for women to be put in charge of running things at times of crisis so they get promoted but only at massive career risk. And while I've been on the receiving end of these phenomena, I realise that I, too, have a tendency to think of women in power as stupid or lightweight when I don't agree with them. At heart, our society tends to judge women leaders as less legitimate, and as a result to question them more critically every step of the way. This is cultural sexism, an unconscious bias threatening the progress of women that is harder to fight than misogyny, because it's harder to see.

The question, then, is what to do? No good will come of anger or victimhood. Even Gillard doesn't believe that her prime ministership ended purely, or even primarily, because of sexism, so if feminists argue that case, we deal ourselves out of the debate straightaway.

We should take heart that the misogynists in our midst are by and large yesterday's men – a bunch of miserable old coots muttering about harlots because it's better than talking about erectile dysfunction. Their anger often emerges around retirement time and is associated, it would seem, with fear of irrelevance. Of the protagonists discussed in Goldsworthy's essay, Larry Pickering is a serial bankrupt whose celebrity star has well and truly faded. And while Alan Jones has survived certain public ignominy before, the descent of the barnstorming run on Canberra he championed into a pathetic "convoy of no consequence" must, even by his standards, have been downright embarrassing.

We could fight all day with the lunatic fringe, but really it's mainstream attitudes that need changing. That's hard work, but not beyond the fabulous progressive women of Australia and the feminist men who support them.

The first step, in my view, is quiet reflection. Australians need to ask themselves why women have not yet gained equality, and whether our own cultural sexism may have something to do with it. The second step is to stand up: to name sexism when we see it – to put away forever the idea that it just has to be tolerated if you want to make it. And the third is to back those women who have a crack – even in Australia in 2013, for a woman to put herself forward is an act of courage.

Gillard ought to be right when she says that her experience as prime minister will make it easier for the women who follow, but this will only be the case if, as a nation, we reflect and we try. To borrow my favourite Gillard expression, let's give it "a red hot go!"

Rachel Nolan

Sara Dowse

Unfair as it is to the author and her subject, my initial response to this insightful and elegantly composed essay was one of utter dismay. It's not that I was naive enough to think that the movement my generation swung into back in the 1970s was going to take us to our destination anytime soon. We were the very ones, as I remember, to decry the fatuous assertion that by the 1990s we had entered some kind of "post-feminist" nirvana. The "longest revolution" is what Juliet Mitchell once called it, and millennia of female subjection showed only too conclusively that there was little reason to argue with her on that. The patriarchy had been with us since the earliest records of history. In the days when it was the thing to do, we readily characterised the particular version we lived under as patriarchal capitalism. Again, I see no reason to dispute this.

But this is the analytical side of me speaking. What dismayed me most about Anna Goldsworthy's essay was more personal, more like: oh, no, not again. I had fought those battles and, truth be told, my heart wasn't in fighting them over again. Halfway through my eighth decade, I guess I'd been living as if one could be retired from feminism, and here I was, responding, though kicking and screaming, to the ancient call. An old friend, who shared with me that gruelling moment of femocracy under Whitlam and Fraser, used to joke that on our deathbeds we'd be ordered to come up with yet another submission on child care. A joke then; now, I realise she was more prescient than either of us could have known.

Goldsworthy doesn't speak about child care, or much about economics. Her focus is on words and images. I would be the last person to suggest that these aren't important, but to me the lack of an economic perspective does leave a hole in the fabric of her argument. This is something I'll get back to. For now, I'll deal with her contentions on her own terms.

The word Goldsworthy focuses most of her attention on is, unsurprisingly, misogyny – a word that's blazed on our political horizon with the firepower of a thousand hand grenades. From the moment Julia Gillard lit the fuse with her October 2012 parliamentary speech lambasting Tony Abbott for daring to propose that her support of Peter Slipper was misogynist, the word crackled over the airwaves and the YouTube representation of her denouncement spread across the world. "I will not be lectured about sexism and misogyny by this man! I will not!" Misogyny, though, at least as I had understood it, wasn't exactly what Gillard meant. Misogyny to me meant implacable hatred of women, a hatred seethed in deep revulsion, something difficult to charge Abbott with, although his views on women's place in society certainly have come across as sexist. But misogyny now, I recognise, is seen to be milder than disgust, but a sort of hard-core sexism, and Gillard might even be credited with tweaking that, a change almost immediately recorded in Australia's *Macquarie Dictionary*. Words change with usage, and none of this should matter, except for the fact that we had a tough enough time in the '70s getting "sexism" taken seriously.

That there are deeply misogynistic elements in Australian culture has been acknowledged for years. Almost every second-wave feminist I know of was confronted with it. The Canberra Women's Liberation headquarters in Bremer Street routinely received used tea bags (and worse) in the mail; likewise the women's unit in the prime minister's department, where I worked. That these acts were sick-making goes without saying, but somehow the subtler yet clearly sexist manoeuvres were more difficult to deal with. Patriarchy will always, for instance, find its female supporters and that, undoubtedly, hurts more. (My version of Janet Albrechtsen was a woman whose name I've thankfully forgotten, a bureaucrat promoted as a foil to me, as lovingly groomed and smoothly opaque in argument as the weirdly celebrated Albrechtsen herself.) Gillard had her share of female critics, who carped about everything from her jackets to her earlobes, but I still believe the greatest compliment her admirers paid her was to criticise her honestly for some of her more regrettable policies.

Goldsworthy has concentrated on how we responded to her looks. "We are a visual species," she argues, and it's a matter no woman can avoid. Gillard couldn't, Hilary Mantel couldn't, nor could Gina Rinehart. The irrepressible, messily grey-headed, sneaker-footed professor Mary Beard, however, took on her detractors and was able to shut the bulk of them up. So what does that example tell us? What should it tell us? That it's wonderful to be free from excessive concern about your appearance, to concentrate on being fully engaged in what you're doing? It seems, alas, to have failed at that.

So enters a new generation of women: the Facebook one. Girls who once preened before a mirror now post their Instagram portraits to the world, yet they're no more satisfied with their looks than we were once, grimacing at the impossibly substandard image the mirror flashed back at us. Botox and liposuction, breast enhancement and *vagina straightening* are options considered by girls in their teens as well as their mothers (options that most of them, needless to say, can't begin to pay for, so dissatisfaction remains constant). This obsession with one's image, Goldsworthy argues, is less a matter of narcissism than shame. When I was a teen in Los Angeles, a slew of my Jewish sisters underwent rhinoplasties (remember all those bandaged noses in the classroom scene in Alicia Silverstone's *Clueless?*). It was considered as shameful to look Jewish then as it was to be pimply or fat. That trend may have subsided, albeit the deep shame of being female has stuck.

A perverse naivety, I guess, led me to believe we'd get over all that. I thought that feminism would help. In some ways it did. Along came the '80s, with affirmative action and power suits and rapid promotion and glass ceilings, and all of a sudden it was all right to be everything, brainy and busty too. Skinny was also okay. Gay was okay. Or getting better. But that wasn't the whole of the story. It began to get more difficult for men. In part that was an equalising effect; more importantly, it began to get more difficult generally. Australia had a long economic boom, but one that was characterised by the increasing casualisation of labour, the neglect of skills training, a shrinking public sector, strained infrastructure and a government committed to boosting the population by encouraging women to have babies and stay at home to look after them, through disadvantaging tax arrangements and soaring costs resulting from the wholesale commercialisation of child care. In other words, while dealing with the patriarchy in capitalism, we overlooked the capitalism in patriarchy, and how that would work, among other things, to make scapegoats of us and increase our sense of shame.

Goldsworthy ends her essay tellingly. "One of the messages of the misogyny speech," she writes, "is that we are not done with feminism yet." True enough. It's been exciting as well as dismaying to see feminism burst forth again, in robust health as ever, to hear the old passion in the voices of women like Goldsworthy. But in a way she has missed the point.

Goldsworthy ends by suggesting that feminism "has much to offer our daughters, even beyond equal pay, the vote, bodily autonomy, the right to own property, the right to have an education. It can offer them subjectivity." What she wants is "liberation from the *she* of third person – who is to be looked at, or tagged in Facebook, or poked with things, like a thing – into that magnificent gender-neutral first person. *I. Me.*" But it's disturbing to me that someone who begins her essay with a discussion of words has overlooked the fact that I and Me have also been at the core of our troubles, that we have too much My already – "My Bus," "My Ferry," "My Super" and on and on, ad nauseam. As individuals we are important, but not perhaps as much as we'd like, or are exhorted, to think. This is the trap that fuels consumer capitalism, a powerful source of perennial dissatisfaction and shame. Instead of "subjectivity," Goldsworthy might have used "agency." For that's what feminism has really been about. Instead of falling for "I," we might just start thinking again about "We."

Sara Dowse

Correspondence

Angela Shanahan

Julia Gillard is a heroic feminist lost cause. We will hear about our antipodean Boadicea until the cows come home. Ignored is the fact that Gillard's lefty mates knifed the sitting prime minister, the terrible record of her government, and the appalling opinion polls which brought her downfall and probably that of the Labor government. Gillard's government was a chaotic flop, but Anna Goldsworthy, a cultural commentator and musician of some distinction, does not mention this.

I was tempted to laugh, yawn and cry through Goldsworthy's bizarrely lurid and confused ideological essay on modern misogyny. She starts out trying to defend the obviously indefensible Gillard as a victim of deep-seated "cultural" misogyny, even though Goldsworthy has to admit Tony Abbott is not a misogynist. So it was a false accusation. Nevertheless, Goldsworthy has to find some reason for what amounted to a terrible slander, so she delves into the weirdness of paranoid feminist ideology and the murky depths of modern pornography, basically to justify the failure of Gillard. Talk about drawing a long bow.

But there is worse. All the talk of misogynistic attacks on Gillard conveniently overlooks the fact that Gillard, and most of the other Labor women, have been propelled into parliament by the feminist cabal called Emily's List. She (and Roxon and co.) had every opportunity any woman could possibly have to make the government a success. They even got a head-start. But they failed – just failed.

That is only one strand of this essay, however. Goldsworthy gets really confusing when she jumps from politics and starts to talk about pornography. This is the nasty stuff apparently bubbling underneath the surface of Australian suburbia, corrupting the young, while housewifely types like me float above it, either ignoring this misogynistic filth or living in blissful ignorance of its existence. Anyway, that is the implication of her two specific criticisms of things I have written.

Her first criticism is that I have denied the existence of widespread misogyny. She quotes from an article I wrote for the *Australian* in March 2013: "nobody in the real world thought misogyny was important. And no one thought it was real." This is a classic case of being quoted out of context. This was an article about Gillard's confected misogyny speech – not about misogyny in general. Misogyny exists in the world alright, ask any African woman, but women in public life in Australia do not have to put up with ingrained structural misogyny. To say that they do is, frankly, laughable.

Gillard's misogyny speech was a deliberate and premeditated attempt to slander the leader of the Opposition. It was not, as Goldsworthy says, spontaneous or "off-message." It was part of a long Labor strategy of personal attacks on Abbott, which began with Rudd, targeting Abbott's perceived "problem with women." Points of argument were even rehearsed by Anthony Albanese before Question Time on the day of the speech. The idea was simply for social media to bang on with that one word. The word was indeed the thing.

However, the power of social media is greatly overestimated. I said in the same article that ordinary people are not online 24/7, and even less are they users of Twitter. So even though people who use it were having a great time thinking they had their finger on the pulse, they didn't. They were being used in a deliberate strategy which pandered to their own narrow obsessions, the main one being having their "finger on the pulse." So I also said this:

> her friends in the lefty/feminist/Green blogs and Twitterati who all thought she was just so "our Julia" were wrong. Nobody in the real world, in Rooty Hill or Woop Woop, thought misogyny was important. And no one thought it was real.

The whole episode was also hypocritical. Remember all the fuss about Alan Jones and shame, the uses of which word Goldsworthy analyses at great length, even though it is probably the most commonly used word in parliament? Not only did Gillard appear with Kyle Sandilands, who in a misogyny marathon with Alan Jones would win hands down, but, as I also said in the piece, the woman is a product of Emily's List – a sexist closed shop if ever there was one.

Actually, the press gallery was right at the time. Most people were either puzzled about the attack on Abbott, scornful of a female PM yelling misogyny, or at best indifferent. Meanwhile disillusionment with a government that had caused electricity prices to more than double continued.

But the practicalities of practical politics are obscured and over-complicated by Goldsworthy's feminist critique, which becomes even more obscure and complicated when she moves on to modern sexualised culture and a long examination of disgusting pornography. On this subject I have always been crystal clear. I have said many times previously, in many articles, that we live in a desensitised pornographic world. It is pagan in its treatment of sex.

However, pornography is not only misogynistic. That is a very narrow view. Yes, pornography is indeed woman-hating, but it is also man-hating and child-hating. Pornography is dehumanising, full stop. It robs men women and children of their dignity by commodifying sex and turning people into objects. It is not simply anti-woman, it is anti-person. And it robs the user as well as the used.

Goldsworthy accuses me of being "gullible," apparently because I didn't talk about pornography in the March article on Julia Gillard's speech, but instead stuck to the point. However, what she really doesn't like is that I am not taken in by feminist gobbledygook and neither are many others, particularly young women. I and many others are fed up with the empty, power-obsessed rhetoric of feminism trotted out to cover every failure, both ethical and practical. To claim the moral high ground of feminism while slapping a low accusation on a decent man puts those women to shame. To put it into context, this what I said:

> Disillusion with feminism is not a recent phenomenon. Even when I began to write for this publication fifteen years ago many women were puzzled by that strange anti-family, anti-man feminism that emerged even after women had actually won equality with men. Clever women chafe under the patronising assumptions of feminists, constantly reminding women of their "debt" to the sisterhood. But the real obstacle with the language and the assumptions behind feminism is that women living in the rich comfortable West in perfect equality with men simply don't believe it anymore. Some of us never have (although, like Margaret Thatcher, we were dismissed as not "real"). Worse still, some of us are even identifying with "the enemy" – a man. No wonder the Emily's Listers were at such pains to denounce the Opposition leader as a "misogynist".

Gullible? I am a child of the sexual revolution who observed with a cold eye the results of feminist urging to fling off our sexual inhibitions, ignore the consequences and behave as men behaved. I graduated when girls were forced either to get on the institutional feminist fast-track or be left behind in the kitchen. Unlike almost all the others, I didn't get on the feminist fast-track, but I am now, as a columnist in political and social affairs for over eighteen years, a spokesperson for the ones with no power, who are left behind in the kitchen. Gullible? I am the mother of nine children, six boys and three girls, and I have three grandchildren. It is a practical breadth of experience on life's coalface that stands in stark contrast to the ideological preoccupations of the *bien pensant* new feminists. On the other hand, Anna Goldsworthy is an excellent pianist.

Angela Shanahan

Helen Razer

When Germaine Greer offered up The Female Eunuch, the feminist portion of the nation received it gratefully. Here was a work that not only described great socio-economic and cultural shifts as they were occurring, but also prescribed a little theory as useful accelerant. The author had, and retains, the gift for taking complex thought and delivering it to a broad audience. Anna Goldsworthy, by contrast, is a wonderful pianist.

It's difficult to unpick Goldsworthy's argument as its ambition does not exceed "Some things in the media make me uncomfortable" and "It's okay to be middle-class and still whine about stuff." The proper spot for this sort of debate – such as it is – is a forum no less serious than first-year cultural studies.

This, in fact, is the chief mode of inquiry in Unfinished Business; data take second place to Goldsworthy's ham-fisted deconstruction of erotic fiction, news reportage and television shows made for premium cable networks. Goldsworthy proceeds with a knowledge of the pop culture that seems to be as scant as her knowledge of late feminist theory (don't you girls read Judith Butler these days?). And don't you think, perhaps, that reading "texts" like Alan Jones for evidence of oppression makes about as much sense as looking at the face of a sarcophagus to understand Egypt's contemporary politics?

Worse than cultural studies (yes, worse than cultural studies), the middle-class feminist hive-mind seems now to be engaged in a sort of wan archaeology. This is Destroy the Joint feminism at maximum drone: with hands upon which there is too much time and insufficient hardship, they brush the dirt off shards of vases and say, "Look! Evidence of oppression!"

Lena Dunham is a very talented screenwriter. Caitlin Moran is a very middling columnist. Neither of them have a place in a serious discussion of the way in which unequal sexual relations are reproduced. And they are reproduced. Just not in the way Goldsworthy – an unwitting disciple of the Third Way – thinks.

If you want to look for evidence of sexism or misogyny or whatever it is the girls are calling Patriarchy these days, one need only visit the Australian Bureau of Statistics. It may not be Goldsworthy's view, but it is objective fact that the lives of women are materially different to the lives of men. Some of us old-fashioned feminists just want to ensure that poverty is no longer feminised; that women have equal superannuation; that it does not fall chiefly to women to bear the time and financial cost of raising children. We don't see that boycotting Alan Jones or watching empowering television has any direct role in this.

Goldsworthy presupposes that there is a link between popular media and behaviour; that magazines and such determine and do not simply reflect inequality. Goldsworthy needs to take a left into the sociology section.

I understand the lure of this kind of analysis. I've made most of my living as an arts critic and I would love nothing more than to play a postmodern game of *Where's Wally?* while looking at texts for evidence of the devil. But it's not grown-up. Let's grow up. Let's learn to see where our personal distaste for unwholesome texts ends and our ability to see patterns made of actual numbers begins.

But perhaps I'm only saying this because I'm a misogynist?

Helen Razer

UNFINISHED BUSINESS

Correspondence

Sylvia Lawson

As Anna Goldsworthy understands, there's a younger generation of women who take the hard-fought benefits of modern feminism for granted, and build their lives accordingly. In arguing that the continuing misogyny and sexism she identifies pervade our first-world lives, she acknowledges that they add up to "a first-world problem," which does nothing about third-world poverty or (for example) female foeticide. Let alone, we could add, about that hatred of women, and the deep, inchoate dread of women as students and thinkers, which incited the attempt last year to kill the young Pakistani activist Malala Yousafzai. After that event, it's impossible to read Goldsworthy's essay without being conscious of that wider framework; and it's not enough, from a first-world, 21st-century position, to dismiss the Taliban as lost in the dark ages. We have to recognise that human advancement proceeds very unevenly.

The near-fatal attack on Malala, who was riding a school bus when she was shot on 9 October 2012, was not an isolated incident, but one event in a long continuum. Earlier, the Taliban had succeeded in closing down hundreds of girls' schools; today, Malala and her father, who taught her politics, are still targets; so are the Pakistani media organisations and journalists who denounced the shooting. The day of Malala's speech to the United Nations – her sixteenth birthday, 12 July 2013 – will remain a landmark date. She called for the right to education to be upheld for all the world's unschooled children; not only girls, but boys as well, and including the sons and daughters of the Taliban. In northwest Pakistan, her contemporaries practise feminism at the risk of their lives. Against the murderous phobias they contend with, "misogyny" is hardly the word; and in that framework the term "feminism" itself signals a kind of courage we don't have to reach for – or at least, not for ourselves. That said, the first-world sphere of understanding can't be sealed off from the rest; and that's the limitation on Goldsworthy's argument.

At the end of her essay she makes strong points, citing Germaine Greer, rejecting any notion that the feminist cause is done and dusted, arguing that cultural change is still "unfinished business," and affirming that men too are victims as well as beneficiaries, since "masculinity can be a more restrictive straitjacket than femininity." (Simone de Beauvoir was there before us; she doesn't idealise the lives of men in the working world, but comments recurrently on their own boredoms and frustrations.) Goldsworthy, however, stops with affirming that feminism "has much to offer our daughters … It can offer them subjectivity – but it is up to them to claim it. A liberation from the *she* of the third person … into that magnificent gender-neutral first person. I. *Me*."

This is middle-class individualism, and its liberating value should never be denied; but if that were the whole story, we'd still be struggling in the fog of the feminine mystique. Individualism spurs the young woman on, but it doesn't provide for justice. We get throbs of properly feminist pleasure when Simone Young conducts Bruckner, and Gale Edwards directs *Coriolanus*; and then reflect that in any democracy worth having, their life chances should be shared by girls across the social landscape. Feminism is necessarily a politics, an open politics: the divisions of class and ethnicity cut across its field. The rights of women are human rights; those who claim them will also defend the rights of this country's First Peoples and the rights of refugees. Like Malala, Australian Aboriginal women activists (and indeed their male supporters) insist that education comes first. Given that, everyday misogyny – which, like the weather, must always be dealt with – comes somewhat lower down on the list as a cause. There are indeed the Alan Joneses and all their baleful kin; but they become grotesque; their antics will shrivel and vanish.

Meanwhile, we can profitably look further back than *The Female Eunuch* – great romantic essay that it is – to Beauvoir and *The Second Sex*; while feminist scholars will argue with and against her forever, that book remains foundational. As Beauvoir's thought developed, liberty became linked irretrievably to responsibility. In assaulting patriarchal structures, she pitched feminism, the interests of women as social beings and citizens, against all imperialisms and on the side of liberation. She would have delighted in young Malala's act of resistance, and been appalled that in the twenty-first century it is still necessary. In her responses (along with those of such other activists as Gisèle Halimi) to French practices of torture during the Algerian war, feminism was there, starkly visible, at the centre of the major national question. In the West, through the later 1960s and '70s, feminist interests emerged from and alongside civil rights and anti-war movements; opposition to the Vietnam War was feminist action, not peripherally but at its centre.

What was affirmed there was the right of women to concern themselves with the largest issues at stake, with the fates of nations as well as their own rights to control their fertility, earn money and vote. To think now, for a major instance, about Australia's response to a small flow of boats carrying desperate women, men and children toward our shores. To aspire to direct *Coriolanus*, or to become prime minister. There has been something of a rush to interpret the story of Julia Gillard, but that story is very far from done. In departing – with far greater dignity than any attained thus far by her male opponents – she has left us with everything to think about from her own record, for better and equally for worse.

Sylvia Lawson

Response to
Correspondence

Anna Goldsworthy

I acknowledge that there is a great deal of unfinished business to my Quarterly Essay. In its defence, I would suggest that any essay of 25,000 words is of necessity partial. The feminist soapbox is a highly contested space; a strain of anxiety persists that there is room upon it for one conversation only. *Unfinished Business* makes no claim to document structural disadvantage, or assess the status of women worldwide. Its aims are perhaps best encapsulated by the woman who inspired it. The week of its release, Julia Gillard was ousted as prime minister. In her concession speech, as Michaela McGuire reminds us, Gillard remarked that "the reaction to being the first female prime minister does not explain everything about my prime ministership, nor does it explain nothing about my prime ministership." She suggested that "it explains some things, and it is for the nation to think in a sophisticated way about those shades of grey."

Are these shades of grey worth thinking about? Angela Shanahan believes not. As does Helen Razer, who here maintains that one should not discuss cultural sexism while structural sexism exists. Sylvia Lawson offers a similar reservation, if more mildly expressed. She points out that "everyday misogyny" comes "somewhat lower down on the list as a cause" than the education of young women, as championed by the young Pakistani activist Malala Yousafzai, whose achievements she rightly celebrates.

In the hierarchy of female suffering, many things trump "everyday misogyny." Female poverty remains a far graver problem than the opinions of Alan Jones, but does this mean those opinions should go unremarked? Several correspondents express confidence in the laws of attrition: Lawson asserts that the antics of "the Alan Joneses and all their baleful kin" will "shrivel and vanish"; Rachel Nolan suggests that "abusive porn or Alan Jones … shrivels in the light of day." I remain less optimistic about the natural processes of shrivelling; my modest hope in writing this essay was to apply some of that light of day.

Sara Dowse offers an eloquent and moving account of decades of entrenched sexism. Both Dowse and Lawson are wary of my formulation of female subjectivity, of the whiff of middle-class individualism about the first-personal pronoun. But first person can mean many things: it can speak to the dignity of the individual as much as *Me Generation* or *Generation Me*. While there may be no *I* without *we*, there is likewise no *we* without *I*, which remains a stronger premise for any action than *she*. Dowse makes a case for "agency" above "subjectivity," but agency too has its limits: the relentless *getting on with it* I charted in the essay.

Claiming our place as subjects involves more than *getting stuff done*. It also means owning up to traits deemed unladylike, not least – as Rebecca Huntley identifies – ambition. Huntley makes the point that "in the end some just couldn't stomach Gillard's naked ambition." Female ambition, like female lust, remains a source of disquiet: hence the Lady Macbeth gibes, invoked by Gillard opponents from Pyne to Rudd. Even some of Gillard's defenders seek to remove its taint, with Kerry-Anne Walsh maintaining in *The Stalking of Julia Gillard* that Gillard was a "most reluctant draftee" to the office of prime minister. Is this what is required to rehabilitate her? Nobody ever becomes prime minister without ambition. But there is a significant difference between Gillard's brand of ambition – which ultimately sacrificed itself for the party – and Kevin Rudd's, which would sacrifice the party for itself.

Huntley brings her expertise as social researcher to the subject, making the point that "Twitter is not the public." Angela Shanahan takes this further, with her contention that "ordinary people are not online 24/7, and even less are they users of Twitter." And so we find ourselves back in that other contested space – the *real world* – whose constituents Shanahan, Rudd and even Alexander Downer claim to represent. It is a space further complicated by the widening gulf between those who embrace and reject technology. Some might imagine that Twitter's echo chambers are the only reality; others stop their ears to it entirely – and the approximately 3 million "non-ordinary" Australians who use it.

Similarly, Rachel Nolan is troubled by "academic" and "weird" discussions of online pornography in the context of feminism, the "most mainstream of all social movements." Perhaps this explains her failure to see how "*Unfinished Business* has much to do with me or with other women I know," even as she proceeds to repeat most of its main points: the ongoing existence of cultural sexism; the tendency of women to just *get on with it*.

Shanahan also rebuts the essay with several points I thought I had made clearly: that Gillard's misogyny speech was not "spontaneous"; that Kyle Sandilands is a misogynist. Much of her letter is a valiant self-defence against charges of gullibility: "Gullible? I am a child of the sexual revolution ... Gullible? I am the mother of nine children ..." At risk of puncturing a great rhetorical moment, I feel obliged to point out that no such charges were ever laid. My remark was simply that in her disavowal of both "misogyny" and "feminism" Shanahan appeared "determined not to be gullible." Shanahan concludes with a flourish: "Anna Goldsworthy is an excellent pianist." Razer turns up at the ball in the same frock, no less gleefully. I respectively acknowledge that Shanahan is indeed a grandmother and that Helen Razer is an arts critic, with an admirable familiarity with undergraduate curricula. None of which amounts to a qualification or disqualification from discussing cultural sexism.

As an occasional arts critic myself, and a more than occasional practitioner, I question Razer's blithe characterisation of the relation between media and behaviour as a one-way street ("just ask sociology"). I agree that feminism is and must be much greater than "spot the misogyny." It is not my intention to enlist women as full-time umpires, blowing the whistle at every infraction, real or perceived. But if Razer's concern is truly the conservation of feminist resources, she might reconsider the vast quantities of energy she deploys in her own destroy-the-Destroy-the-Jointers campaign. Playing "Where's the Wally Spotter" may be even more postmodern than playing "Where's Wally," but it does little to end female poverty either. Gillard's pleas for "shades of grey" notwithstanding, black and white remain the preferred colours of our discourse. The accepted positions seem to be that misogyny is omnipresent, or non-existent. What if misogyny is somewhere, some of the time, and sometimes worth remarking upon?

Since the essay's publication, I have been approached frequently by feminists of Dowse's generation, who share her deep weariness that such conversations persist. It is too easy – particularly as a younger feminist – to forget how much has been achieved, thanks largely to women such as Dowse. Much remains to be done, as our correspondents have remarked, in areas ranging from education to superannuation to child care. Cultural change might be a slow tectonic process, but it deserves some attention too.

Anna Goldsworthy

Sara Dowse is a Sydney-based writer who was the inaugural head of the Office of Women's Affairs under Whitlam and Fraser and drafted the ALP policy on women in the lead-up to the election of the Hawke government.

Anna Goldsworthy is the author of *Piano Lessons* and *Welcome to Your New Life*. Her writing has appeared in the *Monthly*, the *Age*, the *Australian*, the *Adelaide Review* and *The Best Australian Essays*. She is also a concert pianist, with several recordings to her name.

Rebecca Huntley is a director of Ipsos Mackay research and the author of *The World According to Y: Inside the New Adult Generation* and *Eating Between the Lines: Food and Equality in Australia*.

Sylvia Lawson writes cultural history, journalism and fiction. Her recent work includes *Demanding the Impossible: Seven Essays on Resistance* and *The Back of Beyond*. She is currently film critic for the online and print journal *Inside Story*.

David Marr has written for the *Sydney Morning Herald*, the *Age* and the *Monthly*, been editor of the *National Times*, a reporter for *Four Corners*, presenter of ABC TV's *Media Watch* and now writes for the *Guardian*. His books include *Panic*, *Patrick White: A Life*, *The High Price of Heaven*, *Dark Victory* (with Marian Wilkinson) and three previous Quarterly Essays.

Michaela McGuire is the author of *Apply Within: Stories of Career Sabotage* and co-curator of the monthly literary salon Women of Letters. She writes regularly for the *Monthly* and *Good Weekend*.

Rachel Nolan was the state member for Ipswich in the Queensland parliament from 2001 to 2012. She held the portfolios of Transport, Natural Resources, Finance and the Arts as part of Anna Bligh's Labor government.

Helen Razer is a Melbourne writer and an occasional broadcaster. She has published four non-fiction books and writes regularly for the *Big Issue* and the *Guardian*.

Angela Shanahan is a freelance journalist, a regular columnist for the *Australian's* opinion section and a co-founder of the St Thomas More Forum.

SUBSCRIBE to Quarterly Essay & SAVE over 25% on the cover price

Subscriptions: Receive a discount and never miss an issue. Mailed direct to your door.

☐ **1 year subscription** (4 issues): $59 within Australia incl. GST. Outside Australia $89.

☐ **2 year subscription** (8 issues): $105 within Australia incl. GST. Outside Australia $165.

* All prices include postage and handling.

Back Issues: (Prices include postage and handling.)

☐ **QE 2** ($15.95) John Birmingham *Appeasing Jakarta*
☐ **QE 4** ($15.95) Don Watson *Rabbit Syndrome*
☐ **QE 6** ($15.95) John Button *Beyond Belief*
☐ **QE 7** ($15.95) John Martinkus *Paradise Betrayed*
☐ **QE 8** ($15.95) Amanda Lohrey *Groundswell*
☐ **QE 10** ($15.95) Gideon Haigh *Bad Company*
☐ **QE 11** ($15.95) Germaine Greer *Whitefella Jump Up*
☐ **QE 12** ($15.95) David Malouf *Made in England*
☐ **QE 13** ($15.95) Robert Manne with David Corlett *Sending Them Home*
☐ **QE 14** ($15.95) Paul McGeough *Mission Impossible*
☐ **QE 15** ($15.95) Margaret Simons *Latham's World*
☐ **QE 17** ($15.95) John Hirst *"Kangaroo Court"*
☐ **QE 18** ($15.95) Gail Bell *The Worried Well*
☐ **QE 19** ($15.95) Judith Brett *Relaxed & Comfortable*
☐ **QE 20** ($15.95) John Birmingham *A Time for War*
☐ **QE 21** ($15.95) Clive Hamilton *What's Left?*
☐ **QE 22** ($15.95) Amanda Lohrey *Voting for Jesus*
☐ **QE 23** ($15.95) Inga Clendinnen *The History Question*
☐ **QE 24** ($15.95) Robyn Davidson *No Fixed Address*
☐ **QE 25** ($15.95) Peter Hartcher *Bipolar Nation*
☐ **QE 26** ($15.95) David Marr *His Master's Voice*

☐ **QE 27** ($15.95) Ian Lowe *Reaction Time*
☐ **QE 28** ($15.95) Judith Brett *Exit Right*
☐ **QE 29** ($15.95) Anne Manne *Love & Money*
☐ **QE 30** ($15.95) Paul Toohey *Last Drinks*
☐ **QE 31** ($15.95) Tim Flannery *Now or Never*
☐ **QE 32** ($15.95) Kate Jennings *American Revolution*
☐ **QE 33** ($15.95) Guy Pearse *Quarry Vision*
☐ **QE 34** ($15.95) Annabel Crabb *Stop at Nothing*
☐ **QE 36** ($15.95) Mungo MacCallum *Australian Story*
☐ **QE 37** ($15.95) Waleed Aly *What's Right?*
☐ **QE 38** ($15.95) David Marr *Power Trip*
☐ **QE 39** ($15.95) Hugh White *Power Shift*
☐ **QE 42** ($15.95) Judith Brett *Fair Share*
☐ **QE 43** ($15.95) Robert Manne *Bad News*
☐ **QE 44** ($15.95) Andrew Charlton *Man-Made World*
☐ **QE 45** ($15.95) Anna Krien *Us and Them*
☐ **QE 46** ($15.95) Laura Tingle *Great Expectations*
☐ **QE 47** ($15.95) David Marr *Political Animal*
☐ **QE 48** ($15.95) Tim Flannery *After the Future*
☐ **QE 49** ($15.95) Mark Latham *Not Dead Yet*
☐ **QE 50** ($15.95) Anna Goldsworthy *Unfinished Business*

Payment Details: I enclose a cheque/money order made out to Schwartz Media Pty Ltd. Please debit my credit card (Mastercard or Visa accepted).

Card No. ☐☐☐☐ ☐☐☐☐ ☐☐☐☐ ☐☐☐☐

Expiry date   /   CCV   Amount $

Cardholder's name   Signature

Name

Address

Email   Phone

Post or fax this form to: Quarterly Essay, Reply Paid 79448, Collingwood VIC 3066 / Tel: (03) 9486 0288 / Fax: (03) 9486 0244 / Email: subscribe@blackincbooks.com
Subscribe online at **www.quarterlyessay.com**